Corporate Social Responsibility

Corporate Social Responsibility

A *Strategic Perspective*

David Chandler

BUSINESS EXPERT PRESS

First published in 2015 by
Business Expert Press, LLC
222 East 46th Street, New York, NY 10017
www.businessexpertpress.com

ISBN-13: 978-1-60649-914-6 (paperback)
ISBN-13: 978-1-60649-915-3 (e-book)

Business Expert Press Principles for Responsible Management
Education Collection

Collection ISSN: 2331-0014 (print)
Collection ISSN: 2331-0022 (electronic)

Cover and interior design by Exeter Premedia Services Private Ltd.,
Chennai, India

First edition: 2015

10 9 8 7 6 5 4 3 2 1

Printed in the United States of America.

William B. Werther, Jr.,
who taught me how to pay it forward

and

William C. Frederick,
who continues to inspire through his pioneering work in CSR
and business ethics.

Abstract

The goal of this book is to detail the core, defining principles of *strategic corporate social responsibility* (*strategic CSR*) that differentiate it from related concepts, such as CSR, sustainability, and business ethics. The foundation for these principles lies in a pragmatic philosophy, oriented around stakeholder theory and designed to appeal to managers skeptical of existing definitions and organizing principles of CSR, sustainability, or business ethics. It is also designed to stimulate thought within the community of academics committed to these ideas, but who approach them from more traditional perspectives. Most importantly, the goal of this book is to solidify the intellectual framework around an emerging concept, *strategic CSR*, which seeks to redefine the concept of value creation for business in the twenty-first century.

Ultimately, therefore, the purpose of this book is radical—it aims to reform both business education and business practice. By building a theory that defines CSR as core to business operations and value creation (as opposed to peripheral practices that can be marginalized within the firm), these defining principles become applicable across the range of operational functions. In the process, they redefine how businesses approach each of these functions in practice, but also redefine how these subjects should be taught in business schools worldwide. As such, this book will hopefully be of value to instructors, as a complement to their work; students, as a guide in their education; and managers, as a framework to help respond to the complex set of pressures that they face every day.

Keywords

business ethics, corporate social responsibility, *strategic CSR*, strategic management, sustainability, sustainable value creation

Contents

Foreword

What is the purpose of a business corporation? For much of the past three decades, observers and even many business leaders embraced the view that corporations "belong" to their shareholders and that the legal responsibility of corporate directors and executives is to single-mindedly seek to maximize shareholder wealth. Today, experts and laypersons alike increasingly recognize this view of business to be both mistaken and harmful.

As a purely factual matter, corporate law does not require directors and executives to try and maximize profits or share price. Although a business must be profitable to survive, corporate law grants executives and directors of business corporations the discretion to pursue any lawful purpose as a business goal. This "business judgment rule" is something that is consistent across almost all legal jurisdictions.

Nor do shareholders own corporations. Corporations, as legal entities, own themselves. Shareholders own shares that are legal contracts with the corporate entity, just as employees own employment contracts with the entity and bondholders own debt contracts with the corporate entity. A firm's shareholder body is an important partner, but only one of many.

The combined effect of these legal realities, which are the products of decades of both case and statutory law, is to liberate executives and directors to pursue a wide range of practices that they believe to be in the best interests of the organization as a whole. In other words, executives and directors are not bound by any imperative to maximize profits for shareholders in the short term, but can seek to sustain the organization over the medium and long term, ensuring that value is created for a broad range of constituents.

This is important because, from a practical perspective, the dogma of "maximizing shareholder value" does not seem to be working out particularly well for the companies that choose to adopt it. In the quest to "unlock shareholder value," managers have sold off key assets, fired valuable employees, leveraged firms to the brink of bankruptcy, and showered CEOs with stock options in order to "incentivize" them to raise the share price. Some have even committed fraud. Such strategies have proved harmful not only to customers, employees, and taxpayers, but to shareholders themselves. Indeed, even as the business sector has embraced the ideology of shareholder value, shareholder returns from holding public equity have declined. Society, as a whole, is worse off as a result.

This book helps explain why. The framework detailed by David Chandler offers a roadmap for building companies that can do more not only for shareholders, but also for customers, suppliers, employees, and society as a whole. The questions: *Who owns the firm?* and *In whose interests should the firm be run?* are central to this quest. Once we successfully challenge the idea that shareholders own the firm, we remove much of the pressure that drives executives and directors to always favor shareholders' interests over the interests of other stakeholders who are often more invested in the organization and more central to its sustained success.

Corporate Social Responsibility: A Strategic Perspective offers compelling arguments against shareholder primacy. In its place, it presents an alternative vision of *strategic CSR* that builds on a foundation of stakeholder theory and takes into account core insights from the fields of psychology and economics to demonstrate that it is in the strategic interests of the firm to respond to the values, needs, and concerns of all stakeholders. Through this approach, firms generate the most value for the broadest section of society.

Corporate Social Responsibility: A Strategic Perspective is a manifesto for business today. It is essential reading for academics interested in CSR, for students interested in business, and for executives who seek insight into the complex web of competing stakeholder interests they must balance every day.

Lynn A. Stout
Distinguished professor of corporate and business law
Jack G. Clarke Business Law Institute, Cornell Law School

Advance Quotes
For CSR: A Strategic Perspective

In the heated debate over whether corporate social responsibility is an abuse of shareholder value or an obligation to the greater good, David Chandler offers an insightful path forward. With his concept of "*strategic CSR*," he demonstrates the reality of aligned business and societal interests. For the academic, this framework allows analysis of the evolving forces facing the firm and constitutes a syllabus to teach the business leaders of the future. For the corporate responsibility practitioner, it provides guidance on how to balance stakeholder interests and optimize value creation. *Strategic CSR* is not a distraction, but is vital to profit generation. By integrating broader stakeholder interests into strategic planning and core operations, the enterprise will thrive in the dynamic and demanding competitive environment that firms face every day.

Bart Alexander
Principal, Alexander & Associates LLC
Former Chief Corporate Responsibility Officer,
Molson Coors Brewing Company

CSR has become a victim of its own success. The concept is now so accepted, entrenched, and all-encompassing that it means just about anything to everyone. With CSR: A Strategic Perspective, David Chandler does a great job of bringing structure and clarity to this broad field, helping the reader to understand what CSR is and is not, and in the process, bringing sense to this broad concept again.

Michael L. Barnett
Professor, Management & Global Business
Vice Dean for Academic Programs
Rutgers Business School, Rutgers, The State University of New Jersey

David Chandler's view of *Strategic CSR* is eye-opening, innovative, and offers a refreshing pathway out of the longstanding tensions between CSR theorists and profit-seeking corporate managers. His Ten Principles underlying *Strategic CSR* are at once progressive and conservative, pro-business and pro-social, instrumentally pragmatic and normatively focused—all in all, a creative blend of hard-nosed corporate profit-making and globally-diverse socioethical cultures. Stakeholder theory, value creation, the free market—even Milton Friedman—are imaginatively reinterpreted and broadened to support Chandler's integration of Strategy and Corporate Social Responsibility.

William C. Frederick
Professor Emeritus
Katz Graduate School of Business, University of Pittsburgh

Everything you need to know about CSR in a practical and very readable format. Terrific book.

R. Edward Freeman
University Professor and Olsson Professor
The Darden School, University of Virginia

David Chandler has made an important contribution with this new book. For too long, terms like CSR, business ethics, and sustainability have been like collective Rorschach Tests—interpreted by people, corporations, and institutions in idiosyncratic, and often revealing, ways. Yet, the ambiguity surrounding such terms—do they constitute obligations or opportunities for corporations—has impeded their effective integration into the corporate DNA. By articulating his Ten Principles of *Strategic CSR*, Chandler makes clear once and for all, that effective CSR must come from within: It is a function of mental models and problem framing. Once executives internalize CSR thinking into their business logic, it becomes part and parcel to good strategy. In short, the best performing companies in the 21st century will be those that figure out how to solve social and environmental problems and make money doing it.

Stuart L. Hart
Steven Grossman Endowed Chair in Sustainable Business
School of Business Administration, University of Vermont

Chandler's CSR: A Strategic Perspective, is a provocative text for our field that models critical thinking not only for students, but for practitioners and scholars, alike. Rather than accept business practices as they are, Chandler challenges us to imagine them as they could, or even should be—an approach from which our academic colleagues often shy away, for fear that the normative might appear merely judgmental rather than acutely critical. His concise and accessible manner belies the complexity and sophistication of the propositions contained in this succinct volume. If decision-makers do not pay attention to Chandler's principles of strategic social responsibility, it is at the peril of their bottom lines.

Laura Pincus Hartman
Vincent de Paul Professor of Business Ethics
Department of Management, DePaul University

In this well-argued book, David Chandler offers a clear, concise, and comprehensive distillation of thinking about CSR, setting up the next phase of research and theory. He re-energizes the field of inquiry and practice by synthesizing decades of scholarly work and then calling us to adopt a newfound perspective on how best to engage companies in making the world better.

Joshua D. Margolis
James Dinan and Elizabeth Miller Professor of Business Administration
Harvard Business School, Harvard University

"Ultimately, the purpose of this book is radical – it aims to reform both business education and business practice," states David Chandler in *Corporate Social Responsibility: A Strategic Perspective.* Does the book live up to such an ambitious proposition? In my view, it does. And does it brilliantly. In fact, this work bridges many differences and misunderstandings that have plagued for years the literature and practice of CSR. By offering a definition of *strategic CSR* firmly grounded in 10 principles derived from the theory and the practical evidence of the for-profit firm, Chandler's book succeeds in reconciling the common, limited views of shareholder interest, profit maximization, (peripheral) philanthropy, shareholder value creation, and business ethics and sustainability with a wide and inclusive approach where all stakeholders, shareholders included, are represented and whose interests are balanced and accounted for. The far-reaching implication of this book is not only for academics and business education. It is also for managers. *Strategic CSR*, as defined by Chandler, is part of strategic planning and core, day-to-day, activities. It is not an option, it is integral to the whole operation of the company. The book concludes with five important recommendations, that the author calls components since they are a condition for success of *strategic CSR*. In sum, this work provides a sound conceptual framework that embraces all stakeholders in the process of value creation for the firm, and offers guidance to management as how to think far off, shifting from short-termism to long-term decision making.

Miguel Athayde Marques
Professor of Business, Católica Lisbon School of
Business & Economics
Former Management Committee Member, NYSE Euronext,
responsible for global CSR

Strategic CSR is both a provocative and a useful volume. Chandler's Ten Principles provide guideposts to ensure rich discussion, careful thought, and a realistic 21st century understanding of the role of business in society. As Chandler has sifted the history of the field, he has returned on multiple occasions to the writing of Howard Bowen who, in the 1950s— more than 65 years ago—argued that the process of reorienting capitalism to better suit the interests of society, in any era, is a complex process that goes to the very root of our social and economic philosophy. The moral framework within which each generation works is reflected in the public expectations that people share. Those expectations are a blend of economic and social purposes, leavened by a moral compass that is forged amidst the issues of the day. David Chandler has helped us understand the process and the principles that ought to guide the managers of today and tomorrow.

James E. Post
The John F. Smith, Jr. Professor in Management, Emeritus
School of Management, Boston University

David Chandler's CSR: A Strategic Perspective will change the way we think about corporate social responsibility. Chandler re-imagines the role of the corporation in contemporary society. He challenges the myth that the corporation exists solely for the benefit of shareholders and rejects the false dichotomy between capitalism and social responsibility. Instead, Chandler presents the most compelling business case for CSR that I have seen. He convincingly explains how the incentives of capital markets can be used to encourage, rather than coerce, managers to adopt positive social and environmental practices—not simply because they are the right thing to do, but because they make strategic sense. In an increasingly noisy debate, Chandler has become an innovative and sensible voice on *strategic CSR*. If you are interested in sustainable business management, you must read this book.

Roy Suddaby
Eldon Foote Chair of Law and Society and Professor of
Strategic Management
Director of the Canadian Centre for Corporate Social Responsibility
School of Business, University of Alberta

Acknowledgments

This book was written at the intersection of two subjects, *strategy* and *CSR*, which, for me, equates to the intersection of two Bills: First, Bill Werther, who taught me much of what I need to know about strategy and how to be an academic; and second, Bill Frederick, whose intellectual depth and generosity continue to shape the field of *business ethics* and will do so for many generations of academics to come. Thank you to you both—I owe you more than you realize.

In addition, this book benefitted from the insights and constructive criticism of many friends and colleagues along the way. In particular, I would like to thank the following people who kindly gave their time and attention to read early drafts and provide feedback: Mark A. Buchanan, Boise State University; William C. Frederick, University of Pittsburgh (emeritus); Laura Pincus Hartman, DePaul University; Joshua Margolis, Harvard University; James E. Post, Boston University; Mark P. Sharfman, University of Oklahoma; and William B. Werther, Jr., University of Miami. While all errors are mine, this book is significantly better as a result of their suggestions and advice.

Finally, I would like to thank the editor of the United Nations PRME Book Collection, Oliver Laasch, who initially approached me to write this book. Oliver does an immense amount of work behind the scenes for which he receives little acknowledgment, but that, cumulatively, has resulted in the excellent book collection published by Business Expert Press (BEP). He, together with the team at BEP, deserve great credit for their foresight in bringing this collection of ideas together in support of the goal of establishing a stronger intellectual framework for more responsible management education practices in business schools around the world.

Epigraph

In the field of modern business, so rich in opportunity for the exercise of man's finest and most varied mental faculties and moral qualities, mere money-making cannot be regarded as the legitimate end. Neither can mere growth in bulk or power be admitted as a worthy ambition. Nor can a man nobly mindful of his serious responsibilities to society, view business as a game; since with the conduct of business human happiness or misery is inextricably interwoven.

Louis D. Brandeis (1912)[1]

Few trends could so thoroughly undermine the very foundations of our free society as the acceptance by corporate officials of a social responsibility other than to make as much money for their stockholders as possible. This is a fundamentally subversive doctrine.

Milton Friedman (1962)[2]

Introduction

Corporate Social Responsibility

What Is Corporate Social Responsibility?

What is *corporate social responsibility* (CSR)? What is *sustainability*? What is the difference between these two concepts and *business ethics*? Is CR (*corporate responsibility*) different from CSR? What does it mean to be a *corporate citizen*? All of these terms have become commonplace in recent years, but beyond a general sense that corporations have some form of obligation beyond their organizational boundaries; what do they actually mean? Are these concepts mutually exclusive or is there significant overlap among them? And, if they are not the same, why is it that we cannot agree upon universal definitions that convey clearly to corporations the set of behaviors that is expected of them?[1]

> Right now we're in a free-for-all in which CSR means whatever a company wants it to mean: from sending employees out in matching t-shirts to paint a wall for five hours a year, to recycling, to improving supply-chain conditions, to diversity and inclusion. This makes it difficult to have a proper conversation about what corporate responsibilities are and should be.[2]

In other words, in spite of a large and growing amount of work that seeks to understand a firm's *social responsibility*, there remains great confusion and inconsistency. Far from the absence of possible definitions, however, as the aforementioned terms suggest, "the problem is rather that there is an abundance of definitions, which are . . . often biased toward specific interests and thus prevent the development and implementations of the concept."[3] As a result, "the CSR literature remains highly fragmented."[4] While there is broad agreement about the idea that firms have a social responsibility, there is little agreement on what that responsibility looks like in practice:

> There is . . . considerable debate as to whether [society] requires more of the corporation than the obvious: enhancing the society by creating and delivering products and services consumers want, providing employment and career opportunities for employees, developing markets for suppliers, and paying taxes to governments and returns to shareholders and other claimants on the rents generated by the corporation.[5]

How can we argue that CSR is important if we cannot agree what CSR is, or at least narrow it down to a reasonable set of definitions?[6] If CSR remains idiosyncratic (different things to different people), then it loses its essential meaning and ability to influence the way we structure the economic order. This confusion suggests the need for additional clarification, and hopefully some agreement, in terms of what we mean when we talk about *CSR*.

How Is CSR Measured?

Central to the challenge of defining CSR is the challenge of measuring CSR—you have to know what something is before you can quantify it. Unfortunately, however, because we have not been able to define CSR, we have also not done a very good job of measuring CSR. And, as a direct result, we do not have a good sense of what a firm's holistic CSR profile looks like. Although we have some intuitive sense of which firms are *good* and which firms are *bad* (based on our individual assumptions and values), we are presently unable to compare one firm with another reliably across all aspects of operations (particularly if the firms operate in different industries). The reason we are not able to do these things, of course, is because they are incredibly difficult. The challenges involved in defining societal expectations and then quantifying those expectations holistically in terms of firm performance quickly become apparent with a simple thought experiment. Consider the complexities inherent in any attempt to parcel out and quantify the impact an individual firm's operations has on the environment:

> Let's suppose changes in average world temperature lead to the extinction of, let's say Blue Whales, and an obscure currently undiscovered insect in the Amazon. What valuation would we place on the Blue Whale, and how would we calculate it? On the potential economic value of products that might be extracted from it? On the basis of what someone would be prepared to pay for its existence to be preserved? And what about the insect we never even heard of? Suppose it might hold the secret of a new pharmaceutical discovery? Or then again, it might not.[7]

While we may be able to agree that the aggregate effect of all economic activity is contributing to climate change,[8] the degree to which it is doing so and what we might do about it remains unclear. In essence, calculating the present-day value of that cost and determining what percentage an individual firm might be expected to pay is extremely challenging. Should a firm be responsible only for the costs incurred during the production of its products, for example, or also for those incurred during their consumption? Should automobile companies be held responsible for the pollution caused by people driving cars or only for the pollution involved in actually making the cars? What about cellphone companies, where there is little cost to the environment during consumption of the product, but the potential for significant damage during disposal? And, what about a firm's supply chain—where does one firm's responsibility begin and another's end? Should a sports shoe company be responsible for the costs incurred during the manufacture of the shoe (even though that process is completed by an independent contractor)? What about the rubber that is used to make the soles of the shoes—is that also the sports shoe company's responsibility, or the responsibility of the contractor who purchases the raw material, or of the plantation where the rubber was initially harvested? There are no easy answers to these questions, which relate only to the *costs* incurred by a firm. What about quantifying the *benefits* the firm and its products provide, which raises a whole new set of challenges? And, perhaps most importantly, how should these benefits offset the costs?

In spite of these complexities (and many more), the idea that firms have a *social responsibility* continues to capture our attention.[9] We remain convinced that this special thing we are talking about, *CSR*, matters. In particular, we remain convinced that CSR matters for a firm to be a success. One way in which this is apparent is our ongoing effort to address the question: *What are the effects of CSR on firm performance?* Because we are as yet unable to measure CSR accurately, however, the vast majority of these studies tend to capture only a narrow slice of a firm's CSR profile (e.g., pollution levels, litigation against the firm, philanthropic donations, etc.); all of which are important, but none of which capture the totality of CSR—a broad construct that encompasses all aspects of a firm's operations.[10] Such studies also tend to measure the effect of these policies on outcomes such as share price variability or short-term profitability, both of which constitute narrow measures of the firm's operational effectiveness. The result is more confusion, with some results showing that CSR helps performance, some showing it has no effect, and some showing that it hurts performance. In short:

> The empirical literature on the relationship between CSR and performance is mixed and fraught with empirical question marks around not just how performance is measured but what it means to "do good." . . . we simply do not understand the causal link between a firm's specific CSR activities and the operational outcomes that can influence performance.[11]

Yet, we continue to believe that CSR matters. It must matter, right? Being *responsible* is better than being *irresponsible.* And it is important for our sense of justice that those firms that are more responsible should be rewarded in some way, while those firms that are less responsible should be punished. But, what if the reverse is true and it is those firms that make the most effort to be socially responsible that are penalized for doing so by stakeholders who fail to reward the behavior they claim to want from firms?[12] Ultimately, if we cannot come up with consistent definitions of good and bad, and then construct a set of measures that capture the extent to which these ideas are implemented in practice, how can we measure whether CSR actually matters?

We need to get this right because erroneous correlations cause deterministic judgments to be made about these essential ideas. If we are honest with ourselves, we would understand that, in spite of large numbers of studies on this topic,[13] we do not yet have adequate data to measure the all-encompassing nature of CSR. On the contrary, there is good reason to believe that not only are we unable to measure CSR, but that the measures we have are also gravely misleading. That would explain why firms like Enron and BP win CSR, sustainability, and business ethics awards shortly before they commit devastating ethics and environmental transgressions. It is also why companies like Kellogg's and PepsiCo are criticized by Oxfam for "ethical shortfalls, scoring low on commitment to improving the rights of women and farmers . . . [and on] transparency," yet, "the following month, they were listed as two of the world's most ethical companies by the Ethisphere Institute and awarded at a gala dinner in New York."[14] As Mallen Baker argues:

> One of the most common questions I still get asked by managers and journalists alike is for figures to show that doing CSR has a measurable and inevitable positive impact on a company's share price, or on its bottom line. It is a mirage, a distraction. Such figures that do exist are based on a fundamentally flawed premise. . . . Not only is there no agreement about what constitutes a good, or a sustainable, company, but there is also no agreement even on how you would measure the achievement of these criteria.[15]

In spite of the apparent futility involved in measuring a firm's CSR profile, does that mean we have to throw up our hands and surrender, relying instead on subjective moral and ethical arguments designed to persuade managers to *do the right thing*? To the extent that we can arrive at a standardized way of measuring what we agree should be measured, then we will be able to compare one firm's activity with another's.[16] Whether those numbers are 100 percent accurate is less important than whether any biases are known and applied equally across all firms. So many of our measurements involve subjective interpretations and assumptions, but are widely perceived as objective statements of fact (e.g., think about how accountants measure brand value or goodwill). Placing a value on the extinction of the Blue Whale versus the potential damage of an unrealized pharmaceutical discovery will always involve some element of subjectivity and debate. Nevertheless, there is a great deal of benefit in being able to construct a relative and standardized measure of which firms add more or less value. Doing so will help us define CSR accurately and in a way that encourages the reforms in our corporations that are essential to building a more sustainable, value-adding economic system.

This pursuit of defining and measuring CSR is essential because the question *What is the role of the for-profit firm in society?* is highly consequential. Whether we are talking about environmental degradation or social cohesion, wealth distribution or global free trade, the answer to this question defines our immediate and future quality of existence. It determines the society we live in and will pass on to future generations. While some people argue that it is impossible to conclude whether a firm is socially responsible,[17] the more essential question is relative (rather than absolute). In other words, it is important to identify those firms that are more or less responsible than others, without needing to make definitive claims of whether a firm is entirely responsible or irresponsible. While recognizing the challenges in doing so, being able to identify the business models that produce more responsible behavior is a challenge that seems to be inherently worth tackling. Yet, the confusion that is sown by inconsistent definitions, partial measures, and the multitude of labels and rating systems that purport to reveal which products and which firms are *green*, or *ethical*, or *socially responsible* serves only to undermine the good intentions of all involved.

We need to agree on a definition of CSR and we need to recognize that, until we can measure this complex construct, we should be careful about drawing definitive conclusions based on unrepresentative empirical studies.

What Is the Business Case for CSR?

If we are able to agree on a definition of CSR and then begin to measure this elusive concept, we would be in a much better position to answer the question: *What is the business case for CSR?* The challenge in answering this question is related directly to our inability to agree on what we want firms to do and to know whether they are actually doing it. Conceptually, the collective failure of advocates to construct a convincing argument in favor of CSR also reflects a fundamental debate that is yet to be resolved—whether CSR should be voluntary or mandatory.

In the absence of a compelling argument built around self-interest, most of the debate about CSR seeks to force firms to act more responsibly. Whether through moral or ethical guilt, normative association, or restrictive legislation, many in the CSR community believe that CSR should be coerced, rather than incentive driven. This perspective is founded on the assumption that managers do not believe CSR to be in the best interests of the firm (and, by extension, themselves) and that, as a result, they are either unable or unwilling to act in ways that benefit society unless compelled to do so.

This book rejects that assumption on two levels. First, the argument that is framed here is based on the idea that it is only firms that incorporate CSR voluntarily into their strategic planning and all aspects of operations that will do so comprehensively and genuinely. And second that, as a result, building this argument around enlightened self-interest is our best hope of introducing meaningful change. Comprehensive and genuine implementation is likely to generate further innovation and creativity (and social benefit), while selective and coerced implementation is likely to result in resistance and obstruction (and social harm). Worse, by compelling CSR, the danger is that it becomes something to be avoided, rather than something to be embraced[18]—a *responsibility* rather than an *opportunity*.[19] The course of human development demonstrates the fallibility of coercion, while the progress our society has made since the industrial revolution reveals the powerful benefits that spring from the pursuit of self-interest. In *free* societies, humans (and, by extension, organizations) are effective at avoiding coercion—we resist efforts to control and constrain our collective productivity:

> The soundest objection to government intervention in business is not that the matter is none of the government's affair, for it is everybody's affair; the essential point is that controls imposed from

without are always less authentic in a dynamic sense than those evolved from within.[20]

A 2014 law passed by the European Union, for example, mandates CSR reporting by large companies. This regulation was driven largely by organizations such as the European Coalition for Corporate Justice, "a network of more than 250 NGOs, trade unions, consumer groups, and academics," which believes that "a voluntary approach would not lead to a more sustainable and fair society" and that "corporate social and environmental reporting must be mandatory to be taken seriously." What such organizations fail to recognize, however, is that legislation is almost always the result of negotiation and compromise and is, therefore, designed to be flexible. As a result, while "some 6,000 large companies will [now] be required to report on their policies on diversity, social issues, and on corruption, as well as the risks they pose to human rights and to the environment, including through their supply chains," loopholes in the law ensure that:

> The requirements will not apply to the majority of large companies. . . . Companies will also be free to choose which indicators and standards they use for reporting. . . . Reports will be audited, but not verified—and no sanctions are in place for companies that fail to comply.[21]

For-profit firms are most efficient when they are acting in their own self-interest. The most effective laws are those that are founded on widespread social support. If such support is widespread, however, then that behavior is generally accepted as normative (and the law is therefore less necessary). Overzealous attempts to constrain market forces, on the other hand, will generate unintended consequences as firms seek to evade artificial limits. As noted by *The Economist*, "Finance has yet to meet a rule it doesn't want to game," while, in general, "[capital flows] to where frictions are lowest."[22] If the party that is the intended focus does not agree with a specific law or regulation, it will attempt to subvert it, however, surreptitiously. In fact, such behavior will often be encouraged by that very same law or regulation, which is, by definition, broad and ambiguous because it is intended to apply so widely. There is a reason why, for example, corporations employ large armies of highly skilled accountants who are paid very well to find ways for the organization to avoid paying taxes:

> The United States income tax laws allow companies to claim they earned profits in countries where they actually had few, if any, operations, but where taxes are extremely low. . . . the U.S. Public Interest Research Group Education Fund and Citizens for Tax Justice, said that 372 of the companies in the Fortune 500 . . . reported a total of 7,827 subsidiaries in countries that the groups view as tax havens. Some of those subsidiaries no doubt do real business. . . . But most . . . are engaged only in the business of tax avoidance.[23]

Whether such behavior is *right* or *ideal* is a complicated discussion that revolves around the roots of human innovation and creativity. Nevertheless, it is central to the framework presented here that any attempt to amend capitalism in a way that encourages more socially beneficial behavior will be most effective when it is aligned with firms' self-interest, which is related directly to economic success. While we can argue that any particular policy is more or less beneficial, it is the contention of this book that we will only succeed in developing a holistic *business case* when we integrate CSR fully throughout operations and create an environment in which it is understood to be in the firm's best interests to do so.

To date, a sufficiently convincing case has not been made to managers that CSR is of strategic value to the firm. The lack of specificity in terms of both defining and measuring CSR suggests the need for a new conceptualization that is grounded in a business-focused perspective—one that is pragmatic, rather than idealistic; one that deals with human nature as we know it to be, rather than as we may wish it were.[24]

Strategic CSR

Together, our failure to answer adequately these three questions (*What is CSR? How is CSR measured?* and *What is the business case for CSR?*)

suggests the need for an alternative approach. The response advocated in this book is the introduction of *strategic CSR*—a reinterpretation of the relationships firms have with their broad range of stakeholders who are fundamental to the value creating purpose of the for-profit firm in a capitalist society.[25] While variations of this concept exist,[26] the goal here is to define *strategic CSR* more comprehensively in terms that better reflect what we know about human psychology and economic exchange. In particular, this book seeks to establish a set of unifying principles that define the intellectual debate around *strategic CSR*, while also providing a program for managers to implement what, up until now, has been a collection of interesting ideas, but has fallen short of a coherent philosophy and plan of action.

As discussed earlier, "After more than half a century of research and debate, there is not a single widely accepted definition of CSR." Importantly, however, although there is no commonly agreed definition, it is acknowledged that there has been a common purpose to all of the work generated in the name of CSR—"to broaden the obligations of firms to include more than financial considerations."[27] The field of CSR and business ethics has long focused on the ends of business—attempting to force businesses to focus on goals other than, or in addition to, profit. The result has been a lot of wasted energy and a large number of premature pronouncements. As Howard Bowen claimed optimistically in his foundational 1953 book, *Social Responsibilities of the Businessman*:

> The day of plunder, human exploitation, and financial chicanery by private businessmen [sic] has largely passed. And the day when profit maximization was the sole criterion of business success is rapidly fading. We are entering an era when private business will be judged solely in terms of its demonstrable contribution to the general welfare.[28]

Urging firms to "include more than financial considerations" as part of their business model is not the purpose of this book and, in my use of the term, it is also not the purpose of *strategic CSR*. The goal of this book is to refocus the CSR debate onto the *means* of business, rather than the *ends*. Demanding that managers expand the goals of the firm, suggests a problem with the ends of capitalism—that is, profit. In contrast, the underlying principles of *strategic CSR* suggest that any problem with capitalism, as currently practiced, is not with the ends, but the means. Seeking profit (which is the best measure we have of long-term value-added) is not the problem; it is the methods by which profit is sought that can be problematic. In other words, it is not what firms do, but how they do it that matters. When rules are broken, costs are externalized, and key stakeholders ignored (or worse, abused), value is broadly diminished. While some firms may benefit from such practices in the short term, the costs are borne by society as a whole.[29]

Put another way, it is the environment in which the firm operates that creates the boundary conditions that define what the *pursuit of profit* means at any given point in time. The *rules of the game* determine what is acceptable and unacceptable in the way that any single business conducts operations. The goal (profit) stays the same and has always been so, back to the earliest markets on the Silk Road; it is the rules that evolve over time and vary from culture to culture. And, it is the more astute managers who understand the current conditions and, when the rules (both written and unwritten) have shifted, who can guide their firms to greater economic success. They understand that abiding by those rules provides the firm with the license that it requires in order to operate and succeed.[30] But, for this relationship to work, it is essential that the rules are enforced. If the rules are enforced, they will determine the outcome.

The business case for CSR, therefore, originates within the firm. It is a process by which those inside the firm interpret the shifting environment in a way that allows their company to be successful. In other words, it is in the firm's self-interest to understand the rules that are constructed by their stakeholders and abide by them. The problem, of course, is that there is no rule book, per se, and the signals that the firm receives on a day-to-day basis are not consistent, but are many, varied, and contradictory. There is a limited market for socially responsible products, for example, but great savings to be made in waste reduction. Similarly, consumers have demonstrated a limited willingness to be more loyal to a company with a reputation for CSR, but employees are more likely to want to work for such a company:

CSR programs provide a competitive advantage in workforce recruitment. According to a study last year by Nielsen, the media company, 62 percent of people surveyed said they prefer to work for companies that have implemented programs to give back to society. A separate study last year by LRN, a provider of compliance management applications and services, found that 82 percent of American workers said they would be willing to be paid less to work for a company with ethical business practices than receive higher pay at a company with questionable ethics.[31]

The key is that the motivation to act is internally generated, based on an iterative relationship with all the different components of society (business and nonbusiness) that create the rules that constitute the social fabric. Laws are one way that these rules are defined for firms (the government is a stakeholder), but only one of many and, as argued earlier, one of the least efficient. More effective are the myriad of signals that consumers, employees, suppliers, nongovernmental organizations (NGOs), the media, and any other invested constituent conveys to the firm through their day-to-day interactions with it. The result is complex and the message is often garbled, but the stakes for everyone involved are high.

It is not necessarily that firms that ignore these rules will immediately fail, but that they will gradually find their degrees of freedom to operate constricted. In this sense, therefore, much of what is meant by CSR can be captured in a progressive approach to management. As new rules are formed and societal expectations coalesce around these new rules, those firms that understand and abide by them (and anticipate future evolutions) will find the conditions under which they seek profit are easier than those firms that resist. This book is designed to detail the principles on which these new rules are constantly being redefined for those managers who are sufficiently sensitive to detect them and react.

In other words, if CSR is to be widely accepted by the business community, *strategic CSR* has to amount to more than merely the strategic implications of CSR.[32] It has to establish itself as a comprehensive approach to business, replete with its own set of assumptions and guiding principles. This will allow *strategic CSR* to not only be studied as a conceptual framework, but also implemented as a realizable set of practices.

Plan of the Book

In order to present this argument, this book is structured around a set of 10 defining principles with which CSR can be integrated into the firm's strategic planning process and across operations. It builds the case that CSR is a strategic decision that is in the best interests of the firm and those who work within it. Following this introduction, 10 chapters present and discuss each of the principles in turn, followed by a concluding chapter that integrates all 10 principles into a definition and discussion of the concept of *strategic CSR*.

The 10 defining principles of *strategic CSR* serve to differentiate it from related concepts, such as CSR, sustainability, and business ethics. The argument presented is a pragmatic philosophy, oriented around a framework of empowered stakeholders and designed to persuade managers skeptical of existing definitions and organizing principles of CSR, sustainability, or business ethics. It is also designed to stimulate thought within the community of academics committed to these ideas, but who approach them from more traditional perspectives. Most importantly, the goal of this book is to solidify the intellectual framework around an emerging concept, *strategic CSR*, that I believe is essential to our future progress and continued prosperity.

Ultimately, therefore, the purpose of this book is radical—it aims to reform both business education and business practice. By building a theory that defines CSR as core to business operations and value creation (as opposed to a set of peripheral practices that can be marginalized), these defining principles become applicable across the range of operational functions. In the process, they redefine not only how businesses approach each of these functions in practice, but also how these subjects should be taught in business schools worldwide.

PRINCIPLE 1

Business Equals Social Progress

In brief: There is a direct correlation between the amount of business in a society and the extent of progress enjoyed by that society. For-profit firms are the most effective means of achieving that progress.

Principle 1 states that business equals progress. In other words, as a general rule, the more business that exists within a community, the greater the economic and social progress that community will experience. Central to the delivery of that progress is the for-profit firm, which has long been one of the best means for humans to channel their innovation and creativity. As Micklethwait and Wooldridge note in their history of the company:

> Today, the number of private-sector companies that a country boasts . . . is a better guide to its status than the number of battleships it can muster. It is also not a bad guide to its political freedom.[1]

In short, society is stronger when capital flows freely and business is incentivized to innovate and compete. This may seem intuitive when we stop and write it down, but the point is not made often enough. And, in its rush to improve an economic system that has already delivered phenomenal social progress, many in the CSR community overlook this fundamental aspect of capitalism. This does not mean that improvements should not be made, but keeping this starting point in mind anchors the framework underpinning *strategic CSR*.

For-Profit Organizations

Broadly speaking, there are three types of organizations: for-profit, not-for-profit, and governmental. There are also hybrid mixes of these three forms, such as social businesses, government-backed enterprises, and benefit corporations. Of these forms, however, only the for-profit firm is consistently able to combine scarce and valuable resources as efficiently and on the scale necessary to improve meaningfully our society and standard of living. This unique position of for-profit firms is enhanced when we consider the challenges we face, the timeframe in which substantive action is required, and the nature of the complexity inherent in what Paul Polman, CEO of Unilever, calls today's "vuca world: volatile, uncertain, complex and ambiguous."[2]

On the one hand, for-profit firms receive much from society that is essential for them to operate—a stable legal system, an educated workforce, a comprehensive infrastructure, and so on. As such, many CSR advocates argue that firms have a broader responsibility to recognize (and appreciate) that they externalize many of the costs that are associated with these benefits. Some of these costs are implicit in the social contract and are a universal good (such as an educated workforce); some of these costs, however, have harmful societal consequences (such as pollution). Either way, firms rely on society to thrive—they, "receive a social sanction from society that requires that they, in return, contribute to the growth and development of that society."[3]

On the other hand, however, society receives much from strong, for-profit firms that operate within a vibrant, market-based economy. Look around you. Virtually everything you can see was made by a for-profit firm. It is for-profit firms that are responsible either for much of the innovation that allows society to progress or for converting the innovations of others (e.g., scientists, artists, and academics) into commercial products that improve our lives. More important than the value added by for-profit organizations through innovation, however, is the efficient means by which they are able to convert valuable and scarce resources into usable products, and distribute those products to those who demand them at the price those individuals are willing to pay. The details of this process (what for-profit firms do and how they do it) define our quality of life and our level of social progress. The recognition of this leads supporters to claim that:

> The most important organization in the world is the company: the basis of the prosperity of the West and the best hope for the future of the rest of the world.[4]

In other words, while firms benefit greatly from a stable and enlightened society, society also benefits greatly from a vigorous, competitive set of for-profit firms. In considering these tradeoffs and tensions, however, it is important to remind ourselves that juxtaposing firms and society in this way, as many in the CSR community tend to do, suggests that firms and society are independent entities. In reality, of course, they are inseparable. Firms exist as part of society in the same way that society is made up of many functioning parts, an important component of which are for-profit firms. Equally, managers, board directors, employees, and shareholders each have additional roles elsewhere in society (e.g., consumers, volunteers, community members, etc.) as well as working together at the same for-profit firm.

In essence, therefore, business and society are interwoven—their interests are aligned and business has as much to gain from a strong and healthy society as society has to lose from a constrained and ineffective business sector. The question, therefore, is not *What do firms owe society?* or *What does society owe firms?* but instead it is the more nuanced debate about *What role do firms play in society?* While social progress over centuries demonstrates the inescapable value of for-profit firms within a market-based system, each firm should be routinely assessed to understand whether their individual contribution is net positive or net negative. Where it is net positive, we need to ask *Is that contribution as good as it can be—in other words, is it optimal?* Alternatively, where it is net negative, we should inquire *How can we introduce incentives to improve performance?* But, each firm's interest lies not in waiting for this evaluation to be imposed externally, but initiating it to ensure its operations meet the ever-shifting expectations placed upon it. Paul Polman understands this iterative dynamic better than most:

> Business simply can't be a bystander in a system that gives it life in the first place. We have to take responsibility, and that requires more long-term thinking about our business model.[5]

Addressing these questions and providing constructive answers, I believe, is the most important challenge our society faces today.

Business Is Ethical and Moral

It is impossible to separate ethics and morals from any aspect of human behavior. Everything we do involves an ethical and moral component and, more often than not, tradeoffs among ideals. These same tensions and pressures exist in business. In the same way that society and businesses are inseparable, all aspects of a firm's operations, to some degree, have moral, ethical, or value-laden inputs and outputs. While we may agree or disagree about whether an employee should be paid a living wage or a minimum wage, for example, there is no doubt that the decision is consequential for the firm, the employee, and for the society in which both exist. As a result, there is an ethical and moral perspective from which the problem can be addressed and about which we can agree or disagree. These same considerations and conflicts extend to all aspects of operations:

> When a businessman [sic] decides whether or not to produce a new product or service, he is helping to decide the range of products available to customers. When he decides whether or not to purchase new plant and equipment, he is helping to determine the rate of economic progress and is influencing the level of employment and prices. When he decides to close down a plant or to move it to another location, he may be affecting the economic future. When he decides to build up or reduce inventories, he may be contributing to inflation or accelerating recession. When he changes his wage policy or dividend policy, he may be influencing both the level of employment and the degree of justice achieved in our distribution of income. When he uses the newspaper, radio, and television for advertising or public relations, he may be influencing moral and cultural standards. When he introduces new personnel policies, he may be contributing toward cooperation and understanding between labor and management or he may be reinforcing existing tensions and frictions. When he transacts business in foreign lands, he may be contributing to international tensions or to international understanding.[6]

Because the relationship between firms and the societies in which they operate is symbiotic, and firms are able to combine resources on a scale and with an efficiency that no other human-invented entity can match, and there is an ethical and moral component to all aspects of business or human decisions, it is vital to understand the role of for-profit firms in society. The behavior of firms (how they do what they do) affects not only our material wellbeing, but all other aspects of our quality of life and, by a large margin, they are the dominant predictor of that outcome—from our experiences at work, to the products we buy, to the air that we breathe: corporations define the lives that we live.

In other words, the for-profit firm is cause both for celebration and concern. It is true, for example, that, as a rule, societies that provide more freedom for their for-profit organizations to operate will experience more innovation and progress than those societies that do not. It is also true that we should expect this relationship to hold consistently, all else being equal. Of course, all else is not equal, which is the reason for writing this book, and today many feel there is more reason than usual for concern. As Sally Blount, Dean of the Kellogg School of Management at Northwestern University, notes:

> Business is the cultural, organizational, and economic superforce in human development. And yet the current state of this social institution is fundamentally flawed: It falls short in its potential to serve our global society. Today's predominant business models drive public companies, for instance, to focus on predictable, short-term shareholder returns that may be detrimental to employees, communities, or the broader social good. They also fail to motivate industries to reduce their environmental impact.[7]

As with many things in life, the relationship between economic freedom and societal progress is not linear. While the correlation is undoubtedly positive, there are limits to the value of untrammeled economic freedom. It does not necessarily hold, for example, that complete freedom for businesses equals maximum societal progress. If we did not have controls on the use of toxic chemicals in consumer products, there is plenty of evidence to suggest that some firms would take advantage of consumer ignorance and use those chemicals, irrespective of the consequences for public health. Similarly, there is a reason why we place restrictions on the marketing and sales of products that are deemed to be socially harmful, such as alcohol and tobacco. There are good reasons why we allow firms to emit only certain levels of pollutants into the atmosphere or waste stream; there are also reasons why we pressure firms to curb their marketing to vulnerable segments of society, such as children, and so on, and so on.

Rampant, unrestrained capitalism is unlikely to maximize value, broadly defined. A capitalist system that is constrained through a series of checks and balances, however, promises outcomes that serve a broad set of interests. Firms have microinterests and societies have macrointerests. A problem arises, therefore, when the interests of the firm and the interests of society conflict. When this happens, those societies with fewer controls over their organizations will still experience a large degree of innovation, but it will likely result in a reduction in overall value as firms innovate and bring those innovations to market in ways that suit their short-term interests, but work against the longer-term, competing interests of society. The optimal situation is to have the interests of the firm overlap with the interests of the broader society, with both parties working to generate constructive outcomes.

Self-Interest and Public Interest

The mechanism by which the interests of the firm and the interests of society become aligned is through the interactions the firm has with its stakeholders—employees, consumers, suppliers, the government, nongovernmental organizations, and so on. For example, if I, as a consumer, decide that I want to shop at firms that do not outsource their manufacturing jobs and I actively discriminate in favor of such firms (even if it costs me more to do so), then I am making a statement about the kind of firms that I want in my society. Similarly, if I, as an employee, decide to work for firms that have a diverse workforce and I actively apply for jobs only at such firms (and avoid applying for jobs at other firms), then I am again making a statement about the kind of firms that I want in my society. Now, if I am alone in imposing those values on firms, it will not alter anything. If, however, many other people make the same decisions based on a similar set of values, then such values will quickly become standard operating procedure across the majority of firms. This means that, while there is no longer a differentiation advantage to be gained for firms that implement these practices, there is a significant disadvantage for firms that resist. So, standards evolve and society progresses (or regresses, depending on the nature and extent of the change).

These values are embedded in the decisions the firm and its stakeholders make as they interact. As these values are applied and enforced by stakeholders across the thousands of interactions each firm has with its various constituents on a day-to-day basis, the interests of the firm will become more closely aligned with the values of the broader society. As long as the firm is willing to pay attention to the needs and demands of its stakeholders (both internal and external), and those stakeholders are willing to actively shape the society in which they want to live, then it is in the interests of the firm to advance that goal (and its own success) by altering its behavior to match the demands that are placed upon it.

In other words, over time, firms reflect the societies in which they operate. As organizations, they are not conscious actors so much as mirrors that respond to the value-based constraints placed upon them. If we loosen these constraints, those looser standards will quickly become apparent in the behavior they encourage. Equally, however, if we tighten these constraints, firms will respond quickly and efficiently—simply because it is in their best interests to do so and they are very good at acting in their self-interest. But such an iterative relationship relies on our vigilance if it is to generate the outcomes we say we desire. Less vigilance is consequential and is something over which we have control.

The logic behind building this argument of empowered actors and fluid checks and balances (which will be expanded over the coming chapters), and encouraging executives to adopt it as a managing philosophy, is that it should face less resistance than attempts to coerce for-profit firms to act in ways that are contrived and then not enforced by the stakeholders who impose them. As noted in the Introduction, a core unresolved debate within the CSR community is whether more socially responsible behavior is best encouraged via mandated or voluntary actions. The resolution around which *strategic CSR* is based (taking into account human nature and centuries of economic development) is that firms are more likely to implement CSR genuinely and substantively if they are convinced it is in their self-interest to do so. Central to this argument is the belief that firms are more likely to avoid or try and circumvent legislation if they are compelled to act.

In addition to the idea of voluntary action being more fruitful than coerced action, building an argument around incentivized self-interest is likely to be more successful because the concept of *moral duty* or *ethical values* (over and above those already enshrined in laws and social customs) is extremely difficult to define and standardize. This is true because an ethical standard is less easily enforced—in a free society, there are no *ethics police*. Who gets to decide which morals and values apply and in what situations, for example? And, if I disagree with those morals and values (i.e., if I live by a different set of standards), why should I be forced to comply with them? What will happen if I do not comply with someone else's ethical standards?

Take the debate over whether an employee should be paid a minimum wage or a living wage, for example. While I may think a minimum wage is an ethical pay level (after all, by definition, it has been determined by government to be a sufficient income), you may disagree and, instead, argue that a living wage is ethical, while a minimum wage is unethical.[8] But, since it is legal for me to pay a minimum wage, as long as there are sufficient workers willing to work at that level, my company will continue to operate.[9] And, since I am providing employment to workers who are voluntarily choosing to work at that pay level, who is to say that I am being unethical by hiring them? What if, as an employer, I cannot afford to pay wages that are any higher? In that case, would it be more ethical if I hired no-one and left those people unemployed? If, however, workers with the skills that I need for a particular job refuse to work for the minimum wage (or consumers refuse to shop there because of the wages that I pay), then the only way my company will continue to operate is if I raise the wages I am offering.

Similarly, is it more *ethical* for me to hire domestic workers in my factory or outsource production to workers overseas? Some would argue that supporting local jobs is an ethical action, since you are helping reduce unemployment at home, at least in the short term. But, who is to say that is more ethical than hiring a worker overseas, who probably has fewer opportunities and access to fewer resources to improve his or her life? Well, there is a good chance that, depending on the job and the industry, the overseas worker is underage. But, even if that is true, the ethics of the decision to allow that individual to work depends on the available alternatives. It would be unethical to hire a 16-year-old garment maker, for example, only if a well-resourced school was a realistic alternative to working. What if, due to financial pressures, however, the alternative to factory work is prostitution? How does that affect the relative ethics and morality in hiring a local person versus outsourcing work overseas? My point, of course, is only to note that *What is ethical?* and *What is unethical?* are highly complex and relative questions that, once you start to understand the context and different perspectives, do not lead to easily identifiable answers. Where there is consensus, societies should legislate that consensus into legally enforceable standards. Where consensus does not exist, however, your ethics and values differ from mine, and result in great variance in behavioral outcomes.

Having said this, it is important to re-emphasize the enlightened approach to management that is central to *strategic CSR*. Managers reading this are taking away the wrong message if they conclude that self-interest is purely reactive—that, as a firm, I will wait for my stakeholders to declare their interests before responding to them and get away with what I can in the meantime. As argued earlier, a core component of *strategic CSR* is that it is the process that matters—not what a firm does so much as how it does it. A firm is established to meet specific needs. As in any competitive market, it pays firms to be slightly ahead of the curve in doing so (in relation to consumer demand and legislative action, for example). As such, anticipating what stakeholders need and will be willing to enforce is likely to be as important in the 21st century as it has been throughout human economic history. Even better, articulating those needs in a way that those stakeholders had not yet envisioned will continue to generate astounding economic success. As Steve Jobs famously said:

> You can't just ask customers what they want and then try to give that to them. By the time you get it built, they'll want something new.[10]

What is clear from Principle 1 is that enlightened managers working in progressive, for-profit firms are the most effective means to deliver the innovation that drives societal progress. What is also clear, however, is that society (in the form of the firm's collective set of stakeholders) has a direct interest in defining (and enforcing) the constraints within which the for-profit firm operates.

Summary

Principle 1 states that *Business equals social progress*. It argues that the for-profit firm is the most important organizational form because it is best able to convert valuable and scarce resources into products that we demand and, ultimately, that raise the overall standard of living. The incentive to innovate is central to this process, but innovation occurs elsewhere in society, too. Irrespective of its origin, for-profit firms excel when they seek to bring such innovation to market. Integral to this process are the multitude of business decisions, each laden with ethical and moral implications, that the firm makes every day. While self-interest is a powerful motivator, value is optimized in its broadest sense when the interests of the firm overlap significantly with the interests of its multitude of invested stakeholders. *Strategic CSR* represents the mechanism by which these interests are aligned.

PRINCIPLE 2

Shareholders Do Not Own the Firm

In brief: Contrary to popular myth, shareholders do not own the firm. Similarly, managers and directors do not have a fiduciary responsibility to maximize shareholder value. Instead, the firm should be run in the interests of its broad range of stakeholders.

As argued in Principle 1, for-profit firms are the most effective way we have devised to advance social wellbeing. As firms are part of society and society is constructed of multiple components, including firms, the interests of the firm and the interests of society are inextricably interwoven. In other words, business is not a zero-sum exchange, but an ongoing reciprocal relationship between the for-profit firm and its various invested constituents. Together, all of these constituents, plus firms, form the broader group that we refer to as *society*. An answer to the fundamental question that we face (*What is the role of the for-profit firm in society?*), therefore, is best achieved when the interests of the firm and its stakeholders are aligned.

This iterative relationship stems from the origins of the corporation and the evolution of this organizational form throughout history. In particular, it relates directly to the introduction of *limited liability* in the mid-19th century.[1] Prior to this point, corporate charters were granted by the state as a privilege (rather than a right) and under strict conditions in terms of the projects that were to be completed (e.g., building a bridge or a railroad) and the length of time the corporation was allowed to exist. Importantly, these projects were determined on the basis of perceived societal need, rather than the ability of the firm to make a profit:

> In the legal environment of the 1800s, the state in the initial formulation of corporate law could revoke the charter of a corporation if it

failed to act in the public good, and routinely did so. For instance, banks lost their charters in Mississippi, Ohio, and Pennsylvania for "committing serious violations that were likely to leave them in an insolvent or financially unsound condition." In Massachusetts and New York, charters of turnpike corporations were revoked for "not keeping their roads in repair."[2]

And, when the specified project was completed, the corporation ceased to exist. In short, the corporation existed at the pleasure of the state:[3]

> In 1848, Pennsylvania's General Manufacturing Act set a twenty-year limit on manufacturing corporations. As late as 1903, almost half the states limited the duration of corporate charters to between twenty and fifty years. Throughout the nineteenth century, legislatures revoked charters when the corporation wasn't deemed to be fulfilling its responsibilities.[4]

It is because the fundamental legitimacy of the corporation is grounded in these societal origins (i.e., invented to serve society's needs) that, ultimately, *business* is a social exercise. The introduction of limited liability, however, led directly to a shift in the operating principles of the firm. As profit became the primary purpose, rather than the outcome of a valued and meaningful business, it altered the parameters by which the firm's success is measured. While this shift initially generated many benefits, it has become detrimental over time. Specifically, executives today operate under the assumption that the firm's primary obligation is no longer to the state or society, but instead that it has a legal responsibility to operate in the interests of its owners—its shareholders. While this *belief* that shareholders own the firm is widely shared, there is compelling evidence to suggest it is a social construction, rather than a legally defined *fact*:[5]

> Conceiving of public shareholders as "owners" may in some instances by a helpful metaphor, but it is never an accurate description of their rights under corporate law. Shareholders possess none of the incidents of ownership of a corporation—neither the right

of possession, nor the right of control, nor the right of exclusion—and thus "have no more claim to intrinsic ownership and control of the corporation's assets than do other stakeholders."[6]

Understanding the true nature of the relationship between the firm and its investors is therefore necessary to reorient firms to act in the interests of society as a whole. In short, it is essential in order to adopt *strategic CSR* as the managing philosophy of a firm.

Shareholders Own Stock

The great value of limited liability is that it enabled corporations to raise the capital that was needed to finance the infrastructure that fueled the industrial revolution. In particular, limited liability allowed firms to build the railways, canals, and bridges that were central to economic development in the West during the 19th century (particularly in the United Kingdom and United States). As such, at least in its original formulation, the idea of shareholders as a firm's owners had some validity because, while stocks were still traded, the primary purpose of shares was to raise capital and provide a return on that investment from the firm to its investors. Over time, however, the shareholder's role and value to the firm has evolved.

Today, on the surface, the relationship between the firm and its shareholders appears unchanged. Many people believe that the primary function of the stock market is for firms to raise the capital they need to finance their business and, indeed, when firms initially list their shares, this transfer of funds from investor to entrepreneur occurs. In reality, however, this transaction is only a minor part of the stock market's function. Increasingly, it has evolved into a forum for the subsequent trading of those shares, rather than for their initial offering. This shift represents the difference between a trade for which the firm receives money (the initial listing) to one where it receives no money (a subsequent trade between third parties).

As a firm's shares continue to trade and a track record of performance is established, the share price increasingly becomes a vote of confidence in the firm's current management team and its future potential. In other words, when I buy a share in Apple, I almost certainly buy it not from the company, but from another investor who is seeking to sell that share. The price on which we agree reflects our respective bets on the future success of the company. I buy at a price that I believe is lower than it will be in the future, while the seller sells at a price he or she believes is higher than it will be in the future. So, we place our respective bets and the trade is made. In the process, however, an important shift has occurred in the primary function of the stock market and of investors who buy and sell shares today not because they expect to influence a firm's strategic direction, but because they hope to profit from the strategic direction that has already been decided by management. Although activist investors occasionally win seats on a board by amassing significant share holdings, these investors are an extreme minority. In reality, most shareholders can only express their opinions about a firm's management by holding, buying, or selling their shares.

The consequences of this shift in the underlying relationship between the firm and its shareholders were identified long ago by academics who invented the agency theory of firm—Adolf Berle and Gardiner Means in their famous 1932 study, *The Modern Corporation and Private Property*.[7]

> In the late 19th century industry had a voracious need for capital; it found it by listing shares publicly on exchanges. The problem with this, Berle observed, was that over time big successful corporations would come to finance themselves out of retained earnings and have little need for investor-supplied capital. So while the ownership structure provided liquidity for shareholders—they could easily exchange rights for cash—it did not give them the authority tied to conventional ownership, because the company did not need it to maintain their support.[8]

Stock markets are neither efficient (in terms of money flows being dictated by complete and freely available information) nor public (in terms of access being equally and evenly distributed). Stock markets have benefits (in terms of liquidity and providing tools to save for retirement), but it is legitimate to question the overall value they provide. This is especially true today as the majority of trades on any of the major exchanges are made by high-frequency algorithms—computers running programs and holding positions for microseconds:

> There are now at least 58 stock exchanges in the United States. . . . By 2009, high-frequency trading was estimated to account for 50 to 60 percent of the market volume.[9]

One characteristic of high-frequency trading, therefore, is the sheer volume of activity. While high-frequency trades "comprise half of all trades on the American market [they] submit almost 99 percent of the orders."[10] Partly this is because the algorithms are able to handle the associated complexity and can arbitrage value in small increments; partly, though, it is because placing a large number of small orders allows high-frequency traders to learn the intentions of other traders in the market and, as a result, trade more advantageously on that information.[11]

In addition to volume, another characteristic of high-frequency trading is speed. By positioning themselves between buyer and seller, high-frequency traders can generate massive profits on very small margins and extremely large volume. Central to this advantage is being the first to market—the value of which is indicated by the extent to which high-frequency traders are willing to invest in order to gain the slightest of edges over the competition:

> [One] group spent $300m to lay a cable in the straightest possible line from Chicago to New York, cutting through mountains and under car parks, just so the time taken to send a signal back and forth could be cut from 17 milliseconds to 13. In return, the group could charge traders $14m a year to use the line. Traders were willing to shell out those fees because those fractions of a second might generate annual profits of $20 billion.[12]

Almost all of these trades are third-party transactions in which the firm receives no capital directly. The overall effect is to drive a wedge between the interests of the shareholder (return on investment) and the managers of the firm (sustainable, competitive advantage). As pools of assets are increasingly managed by a concentrated number of massive investment firms, this wedge grows larger. Take BlackRock, for example, which in 2013 was the "biggest shareholder in half of the world's 30 largest companies" and managed investments totaling $4.1 trillion, "making it bigger than any bank, insurance company, government fund, or rival asset-management firm."[13] Firms such as BlackRock specialize in what are known as "*passive* investment products," such as exchange-traded funds (ETFs), which attempt to mirror (rather than outperform) the performance of the markets, while minimizing fees to their clients.[14] The traders who work for firms like BlackRock have little direct interest in the day-to-day management of the firms in which they invest. By definition, traders that seek to mirror market performance invest in proportion to the size of each firm in the market, rather than caring necessarily whether Firm A performs better or worse than Firm B. In other words, these traders care about the overall performance of the market (as that is the benchmark they are trying to mimic), but whether they hold positions in Firm A or Firm B is less important—they simply move assets from one to the other in response to macromovements in the market as a whole.

The combination of high-frequency traders holding positions for microseconds and massive investment funds holding large, but passive positions is redefining what it means to be a *shareholder*. In essence, John Maynard Keynes's characterization of financial speculation as "anticipating what average opinion expects the average opinion to be"[15] is truer today than ever before. And, when traders act on behalf of investors, "they're actually in the business of convincing other people that they can anticipate average opinion about average opinion."[16] The cumulative effect is for an individual investor to surrender any claim of *ownership* in favor of managerial control. This trend has been apparent for at least half a century:

> Under modern conditions of large-scale production great power over the lives of people is centered in the relatively few men [sic] who preside over our great corporations. Though the stock ownership of these corporations may be diffused, effective ownership in terms of control resides in management.[17]

In response, some concede that, while shareholders do not control the firm, they still own it. But, does ownership not encompass the ability to control? It is very difficult to think of a definition of ownership that also does not include aspects of control or authority over the thing that is owned. In the *Merriam Webster* dictionary, for example, *ownership* is defined as "the state, relation, or fact of being an owner," with *owner* defined as "to legally possess something," and *possess* defined as "to seize and take control of." Similarly, the *Oxford English Dictionary* defines ownership as the "legal right of possession," with possession defined as "the action or fact of holding something (material or immaterial) as one's own or in one's control."[18] Clearly, however, shareholders do not control the firm.

Irrespective of dictionary or intuitive definitions of ownership, what does the law say about the relationship between the firm and its shareholders? Given the extent to which the idea that shareholders are the legally defined owners of the firm is believed throughout society, it would follow that such a fact is unambiguously stated in law and demonstrated via legal precedent.[19] In the place of clarity, however, the evidence suggests there is only ambiguity:

> This argument [that shareholders own the firm] is based on a misinterpretation of the legal position on the issue of share ownership. . . . Once shareholders subscribe to shares in the corporation, payment made in consideration for the shares is considered property of the corporation, and the shareholders are not free to withdraw the sum invested except for payments through dividends, selling their shares, and other permitted means.[20]

Shareholders own shares. A share is a legal contract between the investor and the firm in the same way that employees, suppliers, and others hold legal contracts with the firm. What is becoming increasingly clear is that, while stockholders invest capital in companies (in the same way that employees invest time, effort, and skills), they have no greater claim to ownership of those companies than other stakeholders.[21] And, there is a growing number of commentators, such as Martin Wolf in the *Financial Times*, who believe their claim is significantly less than other stakeholders:

> The economic purpose of property ownership is to align rights to control with risk-bearing. The owner of a corner shop should

control the business because she is also its chief risk-bearer. Risk, reward and control are aligned. Is it true that the chief risk-bearer in [a publicly-traded corporation] is the shareholder? Obviously not. All those who have stakes in the company that they are unable to hedge bear risks. The most obvious such risk-bearers are employees with firm-specific skills. . . . Shareholders, in contrast, can easily hedge their risks by purchasing a diversified portfolio.[22]

Essentially, being a shareholder entitles the owner of that share to a few specific and highly limited rights: They are able to vote (although the practical application of shareholder democracy is weak and narrow); they are able to receive dividends (only as long as the firm is willing to issue them); and they are able to sell their share to a third-party at a time of their choosing. These rights constitute a contractual relationship between the firm and the shareholder, but do not constitute ownership. As noted by Eugene Fama, one of the originators of the agency theory of the firm, "Ownership of capital should not be confused with ownership of the firm."[23]

One of the great advantages of the Limited Liability Company (LLC) form is that the organization is recognized as an independent entity in the eyes of the law (a legal person). As such, the firm, as an artificial person, has many of the rights (although, it seems, fewer of the responsibilities) of a human being, or natural person. It can own assets, it can sue and be sued, it can enter into contracts, and, in the United States, it has the right to freedom of speech (which it exercises by spending money). It is these rights (the right to be sued, in particular) that allow the investors in a firm to have their legal liability limited to the extent of their financial investment. In short, the firm is a legal creation that exists, by design, independently of all other actors "and it is the corporation not the individual shareholders, that is liable for its debts."[24]

This concept of the firm as a legal person is established in the subconscious of society in the same way that the idea that firms are owned by their shareholders is also established. The difference between the two is that the idea of the corporation as a person is legally defined, while the idea of shareholders as owners is not. In fact, the unique legal status of corporations is constitutionally protected. Following the Civil War, the 14th Amendment was passed to protect the rights of recently freed African American slaves. In particular, it stipulates that the states cannot "deprive any person of life, liberty, or property without due process of law." It is via the 14th amendment that corporations appropriated those rights for themselves.[25] In other words, the U.S. Supreme Court has agreed with the argument that corporations are legally similar to real people and, as such, enjoy similar constitutionally protected rights. The fact that the root of this legal status lies in the 14th Amendment, which was specifically passed to prevent the ownership of individuals by others, reinforces the idea that the corporation is an independent legal entity.[26]

A similar legal foundation for the idea that shareholders own the firm does not exist, in spite of the popular perception that it is true. In other words, as even supporters of the notion of shareholder primacy note, "shareholder wealth maximization is widely accepted at the level of rhetoric but largely ignored as a matter of policy implementation."[27] The reason for this is that, even if it was an ideal, "the rule of wealth maximization for shareholders is virtually impossible to enforce as a practical matter."[28] As a direct result, under U.S. corporate law, courts are reluctant to intervene in the business decisions of a firm unless there is evidence of fraud, misappropriation of funds, or some other illegal activity. The law is clear that corporations are managed by the board of directors who have "broad latitude to run companies as they see fit."[29] Although shareholders nominally have the right to vote for directors, nominating candidates is extremely difficult and, once elected, directors are free to ignore shareholder interests. Although shareholders can protest in terms of resolutions at annual general meetings, "only certain kinds of shareholder votes—such as for mergers or dissolutions—are typically binding. Most are purely advisory."[30]

> The principle that a company's directors should have a free hand to manage its affairs can be traced at least as far back as an 1880 New Hampshire Supreme Court decision. In Charlestown Boot & Shoe Co. vs. Dunsmore, directors won a ruling that shareholders couldn't second guess their decisions, including one to skip insurance on a plant that later burned down. The principle has been adopted by many states, including Delaware, where many large companies are organized.[31]

This *business judgment rule* is similar to common law in the United Kingdom, which refers to the board and senior executives as the "controlling mind and will" of the company. This finding can be traced back to a 1957 Court of Appeal decision by Lord Denning, in which the judge made a distinction between the hands and brains of a company:

> A company may in many ways be likened to the human body. It has a brain and nerve centre which controls what it does. It also has hands which hold the tools and act in accordance with directions from the centre. Some of the people in the company are mere servants and agents who are nothing more than hands to do the work. . . . Others are directors and managers who represent the directing mind and will of the company and control what it does. The state of mind of those managers is the state of mind of the company.[32]

The legal relationship between the firm and its shareholders is all too apparent in the event of a bankruptcy—shareholders' claims to the firm's assets lie behind those of bondholders and all other creditors. Similarly, in other areas, shareholder rights are either highly constrained or outright ignored. In theory, shareholders have a claim to the future earned profits of the firm. In reality, that claim is weak, with no legal right to demand the firm issue dividends or buyback shares if it does not wish to do so. Even in one of the most famous corporate law cases, in which the Dodge brothers sued Henry Ford to increase the proportion of profits that were distributed to shareholders in the form of dividends,[33] the court was reluctant to interfere:

> It is recognized that plans must often be made for a long future, for expected competition, for a continuing as well as an immediately profitable venture. . . . We are not satisfied that the alleged motives of the directors, in so far as they are reflected in the conduct of the business, menace the interests of shareholders.[34]

In essence, the reason limited liability is so important (because it enables investors to limit their risk while allowing firms to raise capital from multiple sources) also explains why the shareholder is legally impotent in terms of ownership:[35]

> Corporations are universally treated by the legal system as "legal persons" that exist separately and independently of their directors, officers, shareholders, or other human persons with whom the legal entity interacts. . . . shareholders do not own corporations; nor do they own the assets of corporations.[36]

Contrary to popular myth, as well as widespread belief among executives and directors,[37] therefore, shareholders do not own the corporation.[38] Instead, they own a type of security (a legal contract) that is commonly referred to as *stock*. The rights associated with this stock are highly limited; in reality, the value of a share lies largely in its resale price, achieved via a transaction on a stock exchange based on third-party perceptions of the firm's future performance potential. As acknowledged, even by shareholder advocates:

> Today, . . . there seems to be substantial agreement among legal scholars and others in the academy that shareholders do not own corporations.[39]

Fiduciary Duties

This challenge to the idea of shareholders as the legal owners of the firm is gradually becoming established. This process is aided by a compelling argument that there is weak legal precedent, in the United States or elsewhere,[40] for the idea that managers and directors have a fiduciary responsibility to place shareholder interests over the interests of other stakeholders:[41]

> Contrary to widespread belief, corporate directors generally are not under a legal obligation to maximise profits for their shareholders. This is reflected in the acceptance in nearly all jurisdictions of some version of the business judgment rule, under which disinterested and informed directors have the discretion to act in

what they believe to be in the best long term interests of the company as a separate entity, even if this does not entail seeking to maximise short-term shareholder value. Where directors pursue the latter goal, it is usually a product not of legal obligation, but of the pressures imposed on them by financial markets, activist shareholders, the threat of a hostile takeover and/or stock-based compensation schemes.[42]

This core concept within corporate law of deference to directors concerning operational decisions (the *business judgment rule*) is embedded firmly in the United States, as well as other countries, such as the United Kingdom:

> Courts in the United States have on several occasions clearly stated that directors are not agents of the shareholders but fiduciaries of the corporation. Section 172 of the U.K. Companies Act 2006, moreover, requires directors to act in the way they consider, in good faith, would be most likely to promote the long-term success of the company for the benefits of its members as a whole, heeding the likely consequences of their decisions on stakeholders such as customers, suppliers, and community, not simply shareholders. The Law even allows the board to put the interests of other stakeholders over and above those of shareholders.[43]

The legal foundation for the belief in the primacy of shareholder interests rests largely on a single case decided in 1919 by the Michigan Supreme Court—*Dodge v. Ford Motor Co.*[44] In the case, two brothers, John Francis Dodge and Horace Elgin Dodge (who, together, owned 10 percent of Ford's shares), sued Henry Ford because of his decision to distribute surplus profit to customers in the form of lower prices for his cars, rather than to shareholders in the form of a dividend. As noted earlier, however, the value of this case as legal precedent for the idea that the firm must operate in the interests of its shareholders is disputed. As Lynn Stout explains in her analysis of this case, contrary to widespread perceptions and norms, there is no obligation on managers or directors to focus the firm's efforts primarily on maximizing shareholder value:

> *Dodge v. Ford* is . . . bad law, at least when cited for the proposition that the corporate purpose is, or should be, maximizing shareholder wealth. *Dodge v. Ford* is a mistake, . . . a doctrinal oddity largely irrelevant to corporate law and corporate practice. What is more, courts and legislatures alike treat it as irrelevant. In the past thirty years, the Delaware courts have cited *Dodge v. Ford* as authority in only one unpublished case, and then not on the subject of corporate purpose, but on another legal question entirely.[45]

More specifically, Stout's empirical analysis of historical case law provides compelling evidence to support her arguments. Not only was the case decided by the Michigan Supreme Court and essentially ignored in Delaware (where the most important points of U.S. corporate law are established), but the legal precedent it represents is more properly understood as a question of the relative responsibilities of majority shareholders (in this case, Ford) toward minority shareholders (in this case, the Dodge brothers).[46] As a result, Stout argues that "we should stop teaching *Dodge v. Ford*"[47] in our universities and business schools as support for a perceived obligation that is neither legally required nor operationally necessary:

> United States corporate law does not, and never has, required directors of public corporations to maximize either share price or shareholder wealth. To the contrary, as long as boards do not use their power to enrich themselves, the law gives them a wide range of discretion to run public corporations with other goals in mind, including growing the firm, creating quality products, protecting employees, and serving the public interest.[48]

Even among those who argue that *Dodge v. Ford* is a more meaningful statement of legal precedent,[49] there is a recognition of the absence of support for a relationship that most people assume is *legally defined* and, as such, compels a fiduciary responsibility:

> The goal of profit maximization is to corporate law what observations about the weather are in ordinary conversation. Everybody talks about it, including judges, but with the lone exception of *Dodge v. Ford*, nobody actually does anything about it.[50]

There is even precedent to suggest that courts will favor the firm's directors over shareholders when the investors have been deceived, basing investment decisions on the firm's publicly stated goals, even if those statements later turn out to be false.[51] A lack of competence or an honest mistake are not sufficient to override the courts' reluctance to interfere with the running of the firm. Unless it can be proved that the directors acted dishonestly or with the intention to deceive, the business will be allowed to rise or fall on the basis of its operational decisions. Although this issue has been studied and debated by corporate legal scholars, however, it is less well known in the business school. This is important and should change:

> Oddly, no previous management research has looked at what the legal literature says about [shareholder control of the firm], so we conducted a systematic analysis of a century's worth of legal theory and precedent. It turns out that the law provides a surprisingly clear answer: Shareholders do not own the corporation, which is an autonomous legal person. What's more, when directors go against shareholder wishes—even when a loss in value is documented—courts side with directors the vast majority of the time. Shareholders seem to get this. They've tried to unseat directors through lawsuits just 24 times in large corporations over the past 20 years; they've succeeded only eight times. In short, directors are to a great extent autonomous.[52]

Shareholders Versus Stakeholders

Contrary to popular myth, therefore, shareholders do not own the firm and directors do not have a fiduciary responsibility to act primarily in their interests. As a result, a growing number of corporate legal scholars argue for a return to the driving purpose of a firm being to meet the needs of society, broadly defined. Central to this argument is the idea that firms seek to return value over the medium to long term among all of their stakeholders and avoid the recent trend of focusing disproportionately on short-term returns to shareholders. The reason why such a narrow focus is counter-productive is that it privileges the interests of a minority (shareholders) over the majority (everyone else)[53] in ways that often do not even benefit the firm.

Pressures from shareholders to maximize results in the short term can be expressed internally within the firm in many ways,[54] "including lower expenditures on research and development, an excessive focus on acquisitions rather than organic growth, underinvestment in long-term projects, and the adoption of executive remuneration structures that reward short rather than long-term performance."[55] The overall effect is to skew the firm's priorities in all aspects of decision making. Why invest for the medium to long term, for example, when that expenditure will diminish the chances of achieving the more immediate priority—short-term profits? Cutting long-term costs, such as R&D or safety and preventative measures has the desired effect of increasing profits today, which is then reflected in a higher share price.[56] While this immediate accounting profit placates those investors who have a short-term outlook, such actions constrain the firm's medium to long-term operations.

In order to manage the firm based on a more sustainable business model, one of the most important changes managers must make is to adopt a broader stakeholder perspective. The difference from the CEO's perspective centers on whether the goal is to maximize performance in the short term (the average tenure for a Fortune 500 CEO is about three and a half years) or to preserve the organization for the foreseeable future (10, 15, 20, or more years from now). The focus should be on what Gus Levy, former senior partner of Goldman Sachs, characterized as being "long-term greedy"[57]—the willingness to privilege long-term value over short-term profits.

To achieve this, an important step is for firms to adopt policies that better align executive remuneration with long-term performance drivers (including CSR and sustainability-related metrics).[58] In addition, firms can de-emphasize short-term results by refusing to issue quarterly earnings reports to shareholders: "Over three quarters of companies still issue such [earnings] guidance."[59] Above and beyond specific policy solutions, however, the key is to deconstruct the idea that there is a legal compulsion to operate the firm in the interests of its shareholders. Once this is achieved, the justification is removed for favoring them over other stakeholders (and, with it, the cause of much of the short-term focus of our economic system):

> As a theoretical matter, the issue of ownership is necessary to a proper understanding of the nature of the corporation and corporate law. As a practical matter, it is an important consideration in the allocation of rights in the corporation: if shareholders are owners, then the balance of rights will tip more heavily in their favor, and against others, than if they are not. . . . Because the issue of ownership has the potential to shape all of corporate law and direct the very purpose of corporations, it is of utmost importance.[60]

The value to the firm in understanding this (removing a short-term focus on shareholder interests, and, instead, seeking constructive, trust-based relations with all stakeholders), is that it immediately alters the nature of the decision-making process. If I see interactions with my stakeholders as one-off exchanges (i.e., a short-term perspective), for example, I am likely to prioritize my own interests during negotiations. If I perceive all my interactions as repeat transactions (i.e., I want to build long-lasting relationships), however, then I am more likely to also care about my partners' interests because, if my partners do not value the exchange, it is less likely that they will want to do business with me again in the future.[61]

In other words, the key focus for debate is temporal. Attempts to maximize profits over the *short term* lead to all the problems that are evident with a narrow focus on shareholder value. If a firm seeks to optimize value over the *long term*, however, many of those problems dissolve and the process of building meaningful, lasting relations with a broad range of stakeholders becomes central to the mission. Firms like Unilever, which stopped issuing quarterly earnings guidance in 2009,[62] understand this and focus on encouraging long-term thinking across all aspects of operations.[63] Amazon is another firm that is altering our understanding of what constitutes a return on investment:

> Amazon seems to have put the "long term" back into Anglo-Saxon capitalism. At a time when Wall Street is obsessed by quarterly results and share buy-backs, Amazon has made it clear to shareholders that, given a choice between making a profit and investing in new areas, it will always choose the latter.[64]

It is fundamental to the idea of *strategic CSR* that, by seeking to meet the needs of as broad an array of stakeholders as possible, a firm holds a competitive advantage in creating value over the medium to long term. Central to achieving this, however, is understanding the true nature of the relationship between the firm and its shareholders and removing the misplaced and inaccurate belief that executives and directors have a legal obligation to make decisions in the interests of shareholders, who are only one of the firm's many stakeholders.[65]

Summary

Principle 2 states that *Shareholders do not own the firm*. In reality, no single group *owns* a large, publicly traded corporation. In addition, managers and directors do not have a fiduciary responsibility to manage the firm primarily in the interests of shareholders. Legally, the corporation is an independent entity (a legal person) with contractual interests. Philosophically, it is the collective effort of the actions and interests of multiple parties, all of whom have a stake in the value creation process. An important step managers can take to reinforce this reality is to resist pressures for short-term performance and, instead, make decisions that are in the medium- to long-term interests of the organization.

Identifying Stakeholders Is Easy; Prioritizing Stakeholder Interests Is Difficult

In brief: Implementing *strategic CSR* requires the firm to operate in the interests of a broad range of stakeholders. While identifying a firm's stakeholders is easy, however, stakeholder theory will only be of practical value when it helps managers prioritize among competing stakeholder interests.

As detailed in Principle 2, shareholders neither own the firm, nor do managers and directors have a legal obligation to run the firm with the primary goal of generating shareholder value. Once managers understand they are free of the mythical obligation to act solely in the interests of the firm's shareholders, they can take a more expansive (and, in terms of the health of the organization, more sustainable) approach to building relations with a much broader range of stakeholders.[1]

This is essential because, although the firm is a legal person, it cannot act alone. A firm is not a sentient actor, but a bundle of contracts (formal and informal) that reflect the aggregated interests of all its stakeholders. If we agree that employees are stakeholders, as well as executives, directors, shareholders, consumers, the government, suppliers, distributors, and so on, then we understand that the firm does not exist independently of these groups. If you take away all the firms' stakeholders (the executives, directors, and employees, in particular), there is nobody left to act—the firm's substance is derived from the individuals that constitute it. This substance comes from the actions initiated by stakeholders pursuing their specific interests (sometimes competing, sometimes complementary) that intersect in the firm's day-to-day operations. This is why stakeholder theory is central to any CSR perspective (really, to any view of the firm), but also explains why it is so important for managers to be able to manage these different interests. To do this, they need to be able to prioritize these interests in order to make decisions that sustain the firm over the long term.

Stakeholder Theory[2]

Contemporary stakeholder theory is usually credited to the work of Ed Freeman. In his important 1984 book, he defined a stakeholder in the following way:

> A stakeholder in an organization is (by definition) any group or individual who can affect or is affected by the achievement of the organization's objectives.[3]

While Freeman did much to popularize stakeholder theory, the idea that the businessman has responsibilities to a broad range of constituents predates his work by many years. As far back as 1945, for example, Frank Pierce, a director of the Standard Oil Company (New Jersey) argued that a firm's managers have a duty "to act as a balance wheel in relation to three groups of interests—the interests of owners, of employees, and of the public, all of whom have a *stake* in the output of industry" (emphasis added).[4] In 1951, Frank Abrams, the CEO of the Standard Oil Company (New Jersey), stated that:

> Business firms are man-made instruments of society. They can be made to achieve their greatest social usefulness . . . when management succeeds in finding a harmonious balance among the claims of the various interested groups: the stockholders, employees, customers, and the public at large.[5]

Similarly, in 1953, Howard Bowen discussed the idea of the "participation of workers, consumers, and possibly of other groups in business decisions."[6] In addition, more specifically, in 1964, Eric Rhenman defined the *stakeholders* in an organization as "the individuals and groups who are depending on the firm in order to achieve their personal goals and on whom the firm is depending for its existence."[7]

As is apparent, the idea of the stakeholder has been around for a while. While Freeman did not claim to have invented the concept,[8] his contribution was pivotal for two main reasons: First, he rendered the concept pragmatic in meaning and action for business practitioners, and second, he promoted the concept within the academic community in general, and the field of management in particular. As a result, a stakeholder is widely understood to be a group or individual with a self-defined interest in the activities of the firm.[9] A core component of the intellectual argument driving *strategic CSR* is that it is in a firm's best interests to meet the needs and expectations of as broad an array of its stakeholders as possible.

In identifying and understanding the interests of its core stakeholders, the firm may find it helpful to divide these key constituents into three separate groups: *organizational* stakeholders (internal to the firm) and *economic* and *societal* stakeholders (external to the firm). Together, these three kinds of stakeholders form a metaphorical concentric set of circles with the firm and its organizational stakeholders at the center within a larger circle that signifies the firm's economic stakeholders. Both of these circles sit within the largest outside circle, which represents society and the firm's societal stakeholders.

Within this overall classification, all possible actors fit primarily into one of the three stakeholder groups. First, stakeholders exist within the organization and include the firm's employees, managers, and directors. Taken together, these internal stakeholders constitute the firm's operational core and, therefore, should be its primary concern. Second are economic stakeholders that include the firm's shareholders, consumers, creditors, and competitors. The interactions that these stakeholders have with the firm are driven primarily by financial concerns. As such, these stakeholders fulfill an important role as the interface between the firm and its larger social environment in ways that create bonds of accountability between the organization and its operating context. Third are those stakeholders that constitute the broader political and social environment in which the firm operates. Examples of these stakeholders include government agencies and regulators, the media, and the broader communities in which the firm operates (including nongovernmental organizations

[NGOs], and other activist groups). These societal stakeholders are essential for the firm in terms of providing the legitimacy necessary for it to survive over the medium to long term.[10]

This model of concentric circles indicates the primary association of each actor, but it is important to recognize that almost all stakeholders exist simultaneously as multiple stakeholder types with network ties among each of them, as well as with the firm.[11] A company's employees, for example, are primarily organizational stakeholders. They are also occasional customers of the firm, as well as being members of the society in which the firm operates. The government that regulates the firm's industry, however, is only a societal stakeholder and has no economic relationship with the company (beyond the taxes it levies and the subsidies it pays), nor is it usually a formal part of the organization. The firm's economic stakeholders represent the interface between the organizational and societal stakeholders. A firm's customers are, first and foremost, economic stakeholders. They are not organizational stakeholders (unless they are also employees), but they are part of the society within which the firm operates. They are also one of the primary means by which the firm delivers its product and interacts with its society. Without the economic interface, a firm loses its mechanism of accountability, and therefore its legitimacy, over the long term.

The three layers of a firm's stakeholders all sit within the larger context of a business environment that is shaped by macrolevel forces such as globalization, climate change, and the increasing affluence that is driving development and raising the expectations society places on its for-profit firms, worldwide.

Prioritizing Stakeholder Interests

In spite of its importance to the concept of *strategic CSR*, stakeholder theory can only be of value to the firm when it accounts fully for the dynamic environment in which business is conducted. In particular, while stakeholder theory is conceptually useful for managers in terms of defining those groups that have an interest in the firm's operations, it has been much less useful in providing a practical road map for implementation. There is a reason for this—while accounting for a broader range of interests is a valuable perspective for a modern-day corporation, it complicates decisions more often than not:

> A single goal, such as maximum profit, is simple and reasonably concrete. But when several goals are introduced and businessmen [sic] must sometimes choose from among them (e.g., greater immediate profit vs. greater company security, or good labor relations vs. low-cost production, or higher dividends vs. higher wages), then confusion and divided counsel are sometimes inevitable.[12]

In short, while identifying stakeholders is easy, prioritizing among stakeholder interests is extremely difficult, and stakeholder theory has been largely silent on this essential issue. Partly this is because the process is so idiosyncratic (firms have different stakeholders who see each action as more or less important), but mostly it is because the interests can be so compelling and conflict so often. What is required is a framework that provides guidance to managers on how and when to prioritize stakeholder interests.

In order to address this, it is essential for firms to define their environments in terms of issues that evolve and stakeholders that have competing interests. Accounting for this dynamic context, relative to the strategic interests of the firm, will help managers decide how to prioritize conflicting stakeholder interests. This is essential because stakeholders have claims on activities that range across all aspects of a firm's operations. Stakeholder theory will remain merely an interesting intellectual exercise until it can help tease apart what John Mackey (the founder of Whole Foods Market) points out, in relation to the claims stakeholders continuously place on his company, are a notoriously complex set of demands:

> Customers want lower prices and higher quality; employees want higher wages and better benefits and better working conditions; suppliers want to give fewer discounts and want you to pick up more of their products; communities want more donations; governments want higher taxes; investors want higher dividends and higher stock prices—every one of the stakeholders wants more, they always want more.[13]

Each stakeholder group "will define the purpose of the business in terms of its own needs and desires, and each perspective is valid and legitimate."[14] As such, it is essential for the firm to be able to identify this conflict, and where possible act to mitigate it, because it represents a potential operational threat:

> Some industries—especially energy. . .—have long had to contend with well-organized pressure groups. . . . Many of the world's major pharmaceutical companies have been pushed to sell low-cost drugs to developing countries. Gap and Nike had been attacked for exploiting child labour in the Indian sub-continent. Coca-Cola, Kraft and other food and beverage companies have been accused of contributing to child obesity in the developed world. . . . Companies that do not acknowledge such claims run risks of reputational damage.[15]

The businesses most likely to succeed in today's rapidly evolving global marketplace will be those best able to adapt to their dynamic environment by balancing the conflicting interests of multiple stakeholders. It can even be argued that, at its core, the fundamental "job of management is to maintain an equitable and working balance among the claims of the various . . . interest groups" that are directly affected by the firm's operations.[16] Just because an individual or organization merits inclusion in a firm's list of relevant stakeholders, however, does not compel the firm (either legally or logically) to comply with every demand that they make. Doing so would be counter-productive as the business would be forced to spend all its time addressing these different demands and negotiating among stakeholders with diametrically opposed requests. A key function of the ability to prioritize stakeholder interests, therefore, is determining which stakeholders warrant the firm's attention and when.[17]

The concentric circles of organizational, economic, and societal stakeholders discussed earlier provide a rough guide to prioritization. By identifying the firm's key stakeholders *within* each category, managers can prioritize the needs and interests of certain groups over others. In addition, *among* categories, as a general rule, stakeholders decrease in importance to the firm the further they are removed from core operations.

Implicit in this discussion, therefore, is the idea that organizational stakeholders are a firm's most important set of constituent groups. Organizational stakeholders are followed in importance by a firm's economic stakeholders, who provide it with the economic capital to survive. Finally, a firm's societal stakeholders deliver it with the social capital that is central to the firm's legitimacy and long-term validity, but are of less immediate importance in terms of day-to-day operations.

In seeking to prioritize its stakeholders, however, a firm needs to keep two key points in mind: First, no organization can afford to ignore consistently the interests of an important stakeholder, even if that group is less important in the relative hierarchy of stakeholders or is removed from day-to-day operations. A good example of this is the government, which is a societal stakeholder and, therefore, in theory, less important than an organizational or economic stakeholders. It would not be wise, however, for a firm to ignore the government repeatedly in relation to an important issue that enjoys broad societal support. Given that the government has the power to constrain or support industries in ways that affect profit levels dramatically, it is only rational that firms should be constantly aware of the government's core needs and requests.

Second, it is vital to remember that the relative importance of stakeholders will differ from firm to firm, issue to issue, and time to time. In addition, depending on these factors, the change in relative ordering can be dramatic. As such, addressing the fluctuating needs of stakeholders and meeting them wherever possible is essential for firms to survive in today's dynamic business environment. In order to do this, it is important that managers have a framework that will enable them to prioritize stakeholder interests for a given issue and account for those expectations in formulating a strategic response.

The key to building such a framework revolves around three moving parts: the *firm*, the *issue*, and the *stakeholder*. First, the firm. Any for-profit organization has strategic guidelines that determine the industries in which it operates and the products or services that it produces. In addition, the firm has market goals that outline future levels of performance that it deems both attainable and desirable (such as percentage market share or a particular level of sales). Together, these strategic guidelines and market goals determine the firm's operational priorities. With this benchmark in mind, managers are able to gauge the strategic relevance of any issue that arises.

Second, the issue. The key factor with any issue that arises is the extent to which it is relevant to the firm's operational priorities. There has been some useful work in this area by Simon Zadek (founder and CEO of the consultancy AccountAbility) that firms can use to evaluate which issues pose the greatest potential opportunity and danger.[18] First, Zadek identifies the five stages of learning that organizations go through "when it comes to developing a sense of corporate responsibility."[19] Then, he combines these five stages of learning with four stages of intensity "to measure the maturity of societal issues and the public's expectations around the issues."[20] The maximum danger, Zadek argues, is for companies that are in defensive mode when facing an institutionalized issue, as they will be ignoring something that potentially poses a significant threat to their business. A firm that continues to deny the existence of climate change, for example, falls into this category. In contrast, those businesses that promote industry-wide adoption of standard practices in relation to a newly emerging issue stand to gain the maximum economic and social value for their effort. Even more effective, for those firms willing to take a bold stand on "issues that are contested enough to feel hot, but that have pretty strong consensus from the tastemakers, mavens, and social-media influencers of the day," they both help move the idea to the mainstream, while positioning themselves to reap the benefits when it arrives.[21] Once the firm has established an issue as operationally relevant and worked out what position it favors, the next step is to identify those stakeholders that are affected.

Third, the stakeholder. In addition to identifying the importance of a particular issue, the firm must account for its various stakeholders. A firm's stakeholder relations will vary within stakeholders, but across issues; they will also vary within issues, but across stakeholders. In other words, each stakeholder will have a number of issues that it values. The range of issues will not be valued equally, however, with some prioritized as more important than others. Similarly, for each issue the firm faces, its different stakeholders will have different positions, pushing the firm to respond in one way or another (or another). The firm's ability to understand how important an issue is to any one stakeholder, and how its stakeholders will vary in response to any one issue, will depend on the depth of the relationship already established. It is a key aspect of stakeholder theory in implementation that any firm will be better placed to understand its stakeholders if it has already established strong relationships based on trust. If the firm is contacting a stakeholder for the first time only in response to a crisis, its outreach is likely to be less well received. However, if the firm has an established relationship and is already aware of the needs and positions of the stakeholder, when a crisis arrives, the potential for a value-added solution is higher.

Combining these three factors (the firm, the issue, and the stakeholder) allows the firm to analyze the range of potential responses to any given situation along three dimensions: *strategic relevance*, *operational impact*, and *stakeholder motivation*. Strategic relevance measures how important the issue is to the firm—in other words, how proximal it is to its core competency or source of competitive advantage. Operational impact measures the extent to which a particular stakeholder group can affect firm operations—in other words, either negatively (the ability to damage reputation or disrupt operations) or positively (the ability to help develop new products or motivate employees). Finally, stakeholder motivation measures how important the particular issue is to the stakeholder—in other words, how likely the stakeholder group is to act.

The extent to which a firm should respond to any particular stakeholder's concern with action, therefore, is determined by the interaction of these three dimensions. Importantly, this framework should be embedded within a culture of outreach to stakeholders, which allows firms to understand their evolving concerns, and assess which issues are more or less important to which group. Ultimately, when strategic relevance, operational impact, and stakeholder motivation are all high, the firm is compelled to act, and act quickly, in order to protect its self-interest.

A Practical Stakeholder Model

The combination of the three factors (firm, issue, and stakeholder) along the three dimensions (strategic relevance, operational impact, and stakeholder motivation) determines the extent to which any issue or stakeholder is central to the firm's interests and whether the firm should act.[22]

Importantly, this framework arms managers with a set of tools that empowers them to analyze their operating environment on an ongoing basis. This set of tools can be summarized by a four-step process of stakeholder prioritization:

1. **Identify** the set of stakeholders that are relevant and important to the firm and seek to build long-term relationships with each stakeholder.
2. **Analyze** the nature of each issue as it arises to see how it relates to firm operations.
3. **Prioritize** among the stakeholders and their competing interests and demands.
4. **Act** as quickly as is prudent, attempting to satisfy as many stakeholders, in order of priority, that is feasible.

Utilizing these four steps optimizes the value of a stakeholder perspective for firms. This process can be applied to identify stakeholder concerns on either an issue-by-issue basis (i.e., a single issue and multiple stakeholders) or on a stakeholder-by-stakeholder basis (i.e., a single stakeholder and multiple issues), depending on the firm's strategic interests. The resulting matrix can be used to plot either where multiple stakeholders stand on any particular issue, or it can be used to plot where one stakeholder stands in relation to multiple issues. Importantly, this model is also both proactive and reactive. It constitutes a tool that firms can use either to anticipate or respond to stakeholder concerns in relation to both opportunities and threats. As such, it allows firms to add value by identifying potential opportunities as well as avoid potential harm to operations by identifying potential threats.

A firm that can implement this framework to help it navigate today's dynamic business environment in ways that allow it to satisfy the needs of most of its stakeholders (at least some of the time), will be best placed to succeed.

Summary

Principle 3 states that *Identifying stakeholders is easy, prioritizing stakeholder interests is difficult.* It lays out the broad ideas behind stakeholder theory, which is the backbone of *strategic CSR*. Importantly, however, it also advances stakeholder theory by moving beyond merely defining a firm's stakeholders to presenting a framework that managers can use to begin prioritizing stakeholder interests. It is the intersection of the firm's operational priorities, the institutionalization of a particular issue, and the motivations of each of its stakeholders that determines the need for the firm to act.

CSR Is Not Solely a *Corporate* Responsibility

In brief: CSR will only work if firms are rewarded for acting and punished for failing to act. As such, while CSR includes a *responsibility* for a firm to meet the needs and demands of its stakeholders, the stakeholders themselves have an equal, if not more important, *responsibility* to hold the firm to account.

As illustrated by Principle 3, business is a collective enterprise that is defined by the firm's relationships with all of its stakeholders. A firm that is acting responsibly is seeking to meet the needs of its broad range of stakeholders. In doing so, that firm is also acting in its own best interests, as measured over the medium to long term. But, within this complex web of complementary and conflicting relations, exactly whose responsibility is CSR? The term *corporate social responsibility* misleadingly suggests that the burden rests solely (or even largely) with the corporation.

Corporate Social Responsibility

The entirety of CSR can be discerned from the three words this phrase contains: *corporate, social,* and *responsibility.* CSR covers the relationship between corporations (or other for-profit firms) and the societies with which they interact. CSR defines society in its widest sense, and on many levels, to include all stakeholders that maintain an ongoing interest in the firm's operations. In addition, as interpreted by the majority of advocates, CSR also includes the responsibilities that the firm has to these varied constituent groups.

What this discussion ignores, however, is an understanding of where the motivation for socially responsible behavior comes from. Should corporations act responsibly because they are convinced of the moral argument for doing so (irrespective of the financial implications of their actions) or should they act responsibly because it is in their self-interest to do so? In other words, what is the point of a firm acting responsibly if its key stakeholders do not care sufficiently to pay the price premium that is often associated with such actions?[1] Unless business suffers as a result of the refusal to act, should firms be expected to change?

Two points are worth emphasizing here: First, for-profit firms are efficient organizations, but managers have no special powers to foresee the future. In spite of this, much of the CSR debate has focused on demanding that firms act proactively out of a social, moral, or ethical duty. In other words, managers are being asked to take a leap of faith—that, if they act *responsibly* (whatever that means), business success will follow. The label *CSR* itself talks about the social responsibility of *corporations* without understanding that, often, there are no meaningful consequences for firms that do not act responsibly and that, in contrast, they are often rewarded economically for not pursuing CSR. Because of this, firms are reluctant to risk their future viability implementing a business model (with the accompanying set of products and services) that does not have an established market demand. While every manager seeks to be ahead of the curve; in reality, there is only danger in being too far ahead.[2] It is important for us to remind ourselves that for-profit firms are mirrors of society and, as such, they *react* to stakeholder concerns or needs far more effectively than they *anticipate* those concerns and needs.

Second, having a responsibility to do something means there is a consequence to not doing it. No consequence, no responsibility. In order for a responsibility to be enforced, therefore, someone or something must hold the firm to account.[3] If this does not happen, then compliance will vary according to the individual actor's set of personal beliefs and values. As such, in order for CSR to work effectively, stakeholders need to act. Stakeholders need to shape the behavior they want to see from firms in terms of what they feel is important. They then must enforce these standards and encourage the behavior they seek by backing up their demands with meaningful commitment and actively discriminating in the relations they build. For consumers, for example, this requires people to educate themselves about their purchase decisions and be willing to pay higher prices where the consequences of their demands raise costs. This same approach and equal responsibility applies to all of the firm's stakeholders, such as government (enforce laws and regulations), suppliers (constructive, productive ties), the media (investigative journalism focusing on abuses of power), and so on. By acting in this way, stakeholders convey to the firm the message that it is in its self-interest to act in a particular way, whether it would have done so voluntarily (i.e., in the absence of such pressure), or not.

In short, existing definitions of CSR focus almost exclusively on the responsibilities of business, while ignoring the responsibilities of the firm's wide range of stakeholders to demand the kind of behavior that they deem to be socially responsible. If the firm's stakeholders are unwilling to set these standards for firms and then enforce them, firms instead will respond with whatever behavior finds success in the market.[4]

Corporate Stakeholder Responsibility[5]

The philosophy underpinning *strategic CSR*, therefore, is clear that CSR should not solely be a corporate responsibility. Stakeholders share an interest in optimizing societal-level outcomes that add value, broadly defined. As a result, they carry an equal, if not more important, responsibility to hold firms to account for their actions. The concept of corporate *stakeholder* responsibility is therefore an essential addition to any definition of CSR that fits within the *strategic CSR* framework.

A New Definition of CSR

A view of the *corporation* and its role in *society* that assumes a *responsibility* among firms to pursue the interests of their stakeholders, broadly defined; but an equal (if not more important) *responsibility* among each firm's stakeholders to hold that firm to account for its actions.

The change in emphasis that forms the core of this definition is subtle, but the implication for our understanding of what CSR means is radical. To this end, it is worth keeping two points in mind: First, this reciprocal relationship does not remove the moral and ethical dimensions of business exchange. On the contrary, these factors are embedded in the decisions all stakeholders take in determining which firms to engage with and which actions to endorse. In effect, therefore, this reconceptualization of CSR shifts the role of morals and ethics in the debate away from fixed standards that are imposed artificially on firms, toward the relative values of each stakeholder that, together, constitute the convoluted environment to which firms have to respond every day.

Second, this division of responsibilities should not be seen as a burden, but as empowering stakeholders to create the society in which they want to live. Contrary to how they are often presented, firms are neither inherently evil nor angelic. As discussed in Principle 3, firms should not be anthropomorphized—they cannot be separated from the aggregated interests of their collective set of stakeholders. Brands and companies are inert—it is the people inside them that bring them to life. The for-profit firm is a group of individuals that, collectively, reflects the society in which it is based. In the same way that we get the politicians we deserve (by electing them), the way we (as stakeholders) manage our relations with firms generates directly the companies that dominate our economies. As such, the firm's stakeholders need to uphold the values and behavior that they say they want firms to implement:

> One report showed that ensuring good working conditions would add less than one dollar to the price of a pair of blue jeans. But despite responding to surveys that they care about ethics, shoppers refuse to pay more. In one study, only half of customers chose a pair of socks marked "good working conditions" even when they were the same price as an unmarked pair; only one quarter of customers paid for the socks when they cost 50 percent more.[6]

In short, if we want to change firm behavior, it is incumbent on us to take responsibility for the consequences of our actions and decisions. This applies to all stakeholders (not only consumers), such as the government, as chair of the Securities and Exchange Commission in the United States, Mary Jo White, states clearly:

> Meaningful monetary penalties—whether against companies or individuals—play a very important role in a strong enforcement

program. . . . They make companies and the industry sit up and take notice of what our expectations are and how vigorously we will pursue wrongdoing.[7]

Firms are largely reactive and will respond efficiently to the signals we send. In a system of checks and balances (both formal and informal), it is incumbent on all parties to play their respective roles. To date, firms have been reluctant to change and stakeholders have been reluctant to enforce the leverage they possess over firms. Until firms become more responsive and stakeholders become more proactive, substantive change will be slow in coming.

Stakeholder Democracy

As these boundaries of acceptable behavior are formed, it is the responsibility of firms to adhere to them, but it is also the responsibility of the firms' stakeholders to enforce them. The outcome of this interactive process is akin to a form of stakeholder democracy:

> The duty of business in a democracy is not merely to meet its social responsibilities as these are defined by businessmen [sic], but rather to follow the social obligations which are defined by the whole community through the give-and-take of public discussion and compromise.[8]

In reality, the way that we differentiate between private sector motivations and public sector demands is usually via the pursuit of profit. But, does that really distinguish different types of behavior? Another way of expressing the balancing act between conflicting stakeholder interests is the push and pull of market forces. While markets are normally thought of in terms of exchanges quantified in monetary value, this concept can be expanded to include a firm's relationships with all its stakeholders, but valued in different ways. Each stakeholder brings different resources to the exchange in ways that can be expressed as opportunities or threats to the firm. As the firm responds to these forces, different outcomes are shaped that, ultimately, match the desires of all parties involved. A good example of a company that actively institutionalizes this mutually dependent relationship is Patagonia, whose product lifecycle initiative represents:

> A unique effort to include consumers in Patagonia's vision of environmental responsibility. An internal document articulated that reducing Patagonia's environmental footprint required a pledge from both the company and its customers. The initiative thus consisted of a mutual contract between the company and its customers to "reduce, repair, reuse, and recycle" the apparel that they consumed.[9]

As mentioned in Principle 2, the history of the modern-day company is embedded in its foundations as a tool to serve society's purposes. Although the emphasis in the company–society relationship has shifted over time, the idea that the corporation is a tool that serves society's interests remains fundamentally intact. In short, if capitalism is no longer serving our interests well, it is because we are not using it correctly. More specifically, we are sending firms the wrong signals, and those signals relate directly to our collective values.

The idea that firms are imposing five-dollar t-shirts on us, for example, greatly misrepresents the way markets operate. If we tell firms with our purchase decisions (and materialistic values) that, with our $30, we want to buy six t-shirts at five dollars each rather than two t-shirts at $15 each, then that is what the market will provide. This is not merely an economic decision, however, but one that is laden with values that have monumental consequences for the kind of society in which we live—one that values quantity over quality, material goods over holistic wellbeing, and short-term comfort over long-term sustainability. If, in contrast, we were willing to buy two t-shirts at $15 each, that would have consequences that would revolutionize our economy (fewer workers in the apparel industry, but better conditions and higher quality t-shirts, for example). Just because we can make t-shirts for five dollars each does not mean that we have to—it is a choice that we make. It is essential to the ideas underpinning *strategic CSR* that we understand that our consumption decisions (as in all stakeholder relations with the firm) represent our values in action. Firms are not actively choosing to supply five-dollar t-shirts so much as they are responding to our demand for such products.[10] If we want the market to change, therefore, we are likely to be more successful if we change the collective set of values that the market reflects, rather than trying to change the centuries-old principles on which the market and for-profit firms operate.

In other words, the argument constructed in this book is not an absolution of the ethical responsibilities of the business executive, but instead a call for those responsibilities to be enforced by the firm's stakeholders who, collectively, have the power to shape the organizational behavior they wish to see. The result of a system that is characterized by tension among competing interests, with give and take on both sides, is a more democratic distribution of the overall income or value embedded within that system. As Howard Bowen noted back in 1953:

> In a rapidly growing society, even if industry is predominantly competitive, there is nothing to prevent the society from receiving part of its increasing product in the form of better working conditions, shorter hours, greater security, greater freedom, better products, etc. Gains need not be realized solely in the form of a greater flow of final goods and services. The rising standard of living may consist not alone in an increasing physical quantity of goods and services, but also in improved conditions under which these goods and services are produced.[11]

Increasingly, the tools are becoming available that enable stakeholders to adopt this proactive role. Another way of saying this is that we no longer have an excuse for failing to act. The Internet provides access to the information we need to make value-based judgments on the policies and operating procedures of the firms with which we interact. Moreover, the price of communication has been lowered essentially to zero, which enables us to mobilize in ways that counteract the power previously held only by governments or corporations. The overall effect of the encroachment of the Internet and social media into every aspect of our lives is to cause companies to lose control over the flow of information. The rise of social media has broken down barriers in ways that are changing how stakeholders interact with firms. While firms can benefit from increased communication and data (to increase efficiencies and market-test products, for example), this technology also hands stakeholders a tool they can use to take direct action and hold firms to account. When we demand more and demonstrate a willingness to sacrifice in order to obtain it, the corporation is the most rapid and efficient mechanism to meet that demand. There is a large body of evidence that demonstrates stakeholder activism is effective. *Strategic CSR* calls for an expanded sense of responsibility among all stakeholders to ensure such activism becomes the norm, rather than the exception.

The ideal ecosystem in which business and society coexist consists of a constant back-and-forth between the self-interest of the business minority and the collective interest of the majority. As society's interests evolve, the resulting external pressures on firms increasingly reflect this change. As these pressures rise, it becomes apparent to the manager that his or her self-interest lies in conforming to these external expectations. Similarly, as businesses innovate and introduce new products and services to society that shape how we live and interact with each other, these changes challenge existing norms and expectations in ways that alter how we live our lives. Understanding that all parties in our economic system help identify this point of balance is essential in creating an economic system that optimizes total value.

Within this framework, an ethics or CSR transgression committed by a firm represents a failure of stakeholder oversight—a breakdown in collective vigilance. Whether as a result of lapsed government or media oversight, consumer ignorance, employee silence, or supplier deceit, a *transgression* (which, by definition, is only a socially constructed assessment of right and wrong) occurs when the firm's stakeholders fail to hold the firm to account. In other words, the firm violates our collective determination of what constitutes responsible behavior.

As a mirror to the collective set of values that make up society, however, firms react to the signals its stakeholders send. It is when those signals become mixed or we fail to enforce the behavior we have previously said we want that problems can emerge. The temptation to substitute short-term profits for necessary safety steps, for example, led to a change in culture at BP and a series of serious accidents, from Alaska, to Texas, to the Gulf of Mexico. If the firm's stakeholders had enforced their oversight (e.g., government inspections, partner operating procedures, employee whistleblowers, etc.), these hugely consequential accidents would have been prevented. Even viable companies that produce legal products (such as the tobacco and gun industries often vilified by CSR advocates) exist only as a result of stakeholder support. If we feel these companies do more harm than good, then it is the responsibility of government to make their products illegal or consumers to boycott them. Stakeholders have it in their collective power to shape the firms we want to populate our economies. Companies are not to blame for profiting by selling products that the firm's collective set of stakeholders have said they value.

Rather than favoring a form of unregulated capitalism, which has been roundly (and correctly) criticized for causing economic mayhem in recent decades, the core argument in this book calls for an expanded form of regulation—stakeholder regulation. Rather than rely on legislatures merely to constrain business via restrictive laws (a necessary but insufficient stakeholder action), an effective and comprehensive form of corporate stakeholder responsibility, in which all stakeholders act to hold firms to account, will generate a market-based system of checks and balances formed around multiple interests. As such, this web of complex interests acts as a curb on unlimited power; it also provides unbounded opportunity for the firm that is sufficiently progressive to meet and exceed the expectations of its stakeholders. The ultimate effect will be to ensure capitalism is tailored more toward broader, societal interests, rather than narrow, individual, or corporate interests.

In this sense, *strategic CSR* is not a passive doctrine; it is highly empowering and potentially revolutionary. True, it is working within the current system, utilizing a firm's pursuit of profit and individuals' self-interest to achieve its goals; however, the subtle shifts that it advocates seek to generate very different outcomes throughout society.

Summary

Principle 4 states that *CSR is not solely a* corporate *responsibility*. Instead, a joint responsibility of both the firm and all of its stakeholders is essential if we are to achieve the *socially responsible* outcomes we say we seek. This constant, iterative, evolving relationship reflects the dynamic way in which business and society are inextricably interwoven. But, it is essential that all parties (the business and each of its stakeholder groups) play their part. While firms have a responsibility (founded in self-interest) to accommodate, wherever possible, the needs and concerns of their broad range of stakeholders, each stakeholder group has a responsibility (founded in self-preservation and social progress) to shape a firm's behavior through expectations that it conveys via meaningful action. This *stakeholder* responsibility is equal, if not more important, to the responsibility of the firm.

PRINCIPLE 5

Market-Based Solutions Are Optimal

In brief: In general, market forces generate superior outcomes than alternative means of allocating scarce and valuable resources, such as government mandate. While stakeholders have an interest in shaping the behavior of for-profit firms, the mechanism by which this occurs most effectively is the market.

As indicated by Principle 4, business is a collaborative exercise. It is in society's best interests to encourage capitalism because for-profit firms are able to foster social progress above and beyond any other organizational form in any other economic system:

It's multinational corporations, and not governments or non-profits, that have the vast human and financial capital, advanced technology, international footprint, market power and financial motivation to solve the world's most daunting problems.[1]

It is also in society's interests, however, to shape the economic behavior of for-profit firms. By holding firms to account for their actions, this *stakeholder democracy* ensures that it is in firms' best interests to seek to accommodate the needs and interests of all stakeholders. This system of checks and balances works best within a capitalist economic system, where enterprise drives innovation, which increases productivity:

In Britain, for example, productivity in the private service sector increased by 14 percent between 1999 and 2013, while productivity in the government sector fell by 1 percent between 1999 and 2010.[2]

Imperfect Markets

The core idea around which Principle 5 is built is that markets trump all other known means by which scarce and valuable resources are allocated on a society-wide basis.[3] The beauty of the market, in large part, is its chaotic complexity, where structure somehow emerges out of a multitude of individual decisions that aggregate into the macroeconomic system. As Friedrich Hayek noted long ago:

> We are led—for example by the pricing system in market exchange— to do things by circumstances of which we are largely unaware and which produce results that we do not intend. In our economic activities we do not know the needs which we satisfy nor the sources of the things which we get. Almost all of us serve people whom we do not know, and even of whose existence we are ignorant; and we in turn constantly live on the services of other people of whom we know nothing. All this is possible because we stand in a great framework of institutions and traditions–economic, legal, and moral–into which we fit ourselves by obeying certain rules of conduct that we never made, and which we have never understood in the sense in which we understand how the things that we manufacture function.[4]

Market freedoms are particularly efficient in contrast to government mandate. In part, this is due to the lack of expertise and local knowledge that a central body, by definition, does not have: "Soviet bureaucrats sitting in Moscow, for example, could not possibly know enough to dictate to farmers in individual fields about how to plant their crops."[5] But, it also reflects the powerful ability of the market (and the profit incentive) to mobilize resources and incentivize human creativity to innovate in ways that alternative motivations, such as altruism and public service, cannot match:

> Johnson Controls joined real-estate firm Jones Lang LaSalle to retrofit the Empire State Building for energy efficiency in 2012. The Clinton Climate Initiative and Rocky Mountain Institute also col-

laborated on the project. The groups estimate the project will cut energy costs by 38 percent, saving $4.4m annually and reducing carbon emissions by 105,000 metric tons over 15 years. Given that the building sector consumes up to 40 percent of the world's energy, energy efficiency is key to reducing our energy use. Retrofitting for energy efficiency is good for the world, while also generating profit for Johnson Controls. The power of financial motivation . . . solved this problem.[6]

The cumulative effects of excessive microintervention by governments, as Milton Friedman dryly noted, can be widespread inefficiency and distorted incentives: "If you put the federal government in charge of the Sahara Desert, in 5 years there'd be a shortage of sand." While an exaggeration, to be sure, it is also instructive as a cautionary tale. The history of humankind suggests strongly that, while the government has a vital role to play in delivering certain services (such as national defense) and creating the boundaries within which economic exchanges can thrive (such as a stable legal system of enforceable contracts), it is via the spirit of free enterprise that innovation flourishes and poverty is diminished. In Milton Friedman's words again:

> The great achievements of civilization have not come from government bureaus. Einstein didn't construct his theory under order from a bureaucrat. Henry Ford didn't revolutionize the automobile industry that way. In the only cases in which the masses have escaped from [grinding poverty], the only cases in recorded history, is where they have had capitalism and largely free trade. If you want to know where the masses are worst off, it is exactly in the kinds the societies that depart from that. So the record of history is absolutely crystal clear, that there is no alternative way so far discovered of improving the lot of the ordinary people that can hold a candle to the productive activities that are unleashed by a free enterprise system.[7]

In spite of the obvious power of markets to build wealth and promote social progress, it is also true that, in application, markets are inherently flawed. Markets, for example, have the ability to misallocate resources (the reason why CEOs are overpaid), skew priorities (the reason why education is so poorly funded), and focus on the short term (the reason why stock prices fluctuate randomly). As another Nobel Prize-winning economist, Joseph Stiglitz, notes:

> Perfect competition should drive profits to zero, at least theoretically, but we have monopolies and oligopolies making persistently high profits. C.E.O.s enjoy incomes that are on average 295 times that of the typical worker, a much higher ratio than in the past, without any evidence of a proportionate increase in productivity.[8]

These flaws arise due to the fact that markets (like governments) are enacted by humans. As James Madison astutely noted, on the one hand, "If men were angels, no government would be necessary," while on the other hand, "If angels were to govern men, neither external nor internal controls on government would be necessary."[9] As such, an important contribution of *strategic CSR* is the construction of a framework that allows us to curb our inherent fallibilities, wherever possible.

The inescapable presence of human influence means that many of the theoretical assumptions underlying market interactions are undermined. Markets work best with complete information, for example— that is, accurate information that is freely and equally available to all participants. In the absence of these conditions (i.e., reality), markets become imperfect. The reason why insider trading in shares is illegal is because it directly transgresses on the assumption of perfect information.[10] Unfortunately, imperfect or asymmetric information is the norm. Sometimes this is a result of deliberate manipulation (as in the case of insider trading); however, more often it is due to human limitations (an inability to process large amounts of information, act rationally, ignore sunk costs, evaluate opportunity costs, overcome biases and fears, and so on).[11]

One market that is often cited by supporters as being purer than most is the stock market. Yet, we know from the 2007–2008 financial crisis that the stock market is inherently challenged when it comes to accurately pricing risk. It is not even clear that investors are good at assessing overall value. As Warren Buffett has stated, "I'd be a bum on the street with a tin cup if the markets were always efficient."[12] The prevalence of bubbles and the tendency toward herd behavior demonstrate that psychology and emotion play as large a part in determining stock movements as financial analysis. Buffett's success relies on traders either under- or overvaluing shares as a result of imperfect information and poor judgment, which allows so-called *value traders* to take advantage:

> Mr. Buffett began an investment partnership in 1956 and, over the next 12 years, achieved a 29.5 percent compound return. . . . In comparison, the Dow Jones industrial average rose by 7.4 percent per year during the same period. Then, in 1965, Mr. Buffett took control of a small Massachusetts textile manufacturer and through a combination of buying stocks and, later, buying entire companies, achieved a 19.7 percent annual increase in Berkshire Hathaway's stock price while the average was increasing by 9.4 percent.[13]

An example of the limits of the market in being able to value all goods is evident in relation to nature. Whether dealing with *use value* (natural goods that have a use, such as water) or *nonuse value* (natural goods that do not have a use, but are valued for intangible reasons like their beauty, such as a water geyser), there are market tools that can be employed (e.g., the level of admission people are willing to pay to visit a national park). Arriving at a complete valuation for such goods, however, is challenging.[14] Fresh water is a good example of this. While it is essential to life and is also relatively scarce (and, therefore, in theory, should have a high valuation), its exchange value is limited (the trade value for a bottle of water is low), largely because equal access to it is considered a cornerstone of a civilized society:

> Adam Smith spotted that economics has problems valuing nature. "Nothing is more useful than water: but it will purchase scarce anything; scarce anything can be had in exchange for it. A diamond, on the contrary, has scarce value in use; but a very great quantity of other goods may frequently be had in exchange for it," he wrote.[15]

The bottled water industry, of course, is also a good example of how, even when faced with such limitations, the market is able to overcome them—if incompletely. Equally, the example of access to clean water demonstrates that, because of the flaws inherent in the application of market ideology, some form of constraint is required. As detailed in Principle 4, an ideal constraint in an effective system of checks and balances is empowered and invested stakeholders who are willing to hold the firm to account. This ensures the firm is incentivized to act in the best interests of the collective needs of those stakeholders (which, altogether, constitute society), rather than the interests of a narrow select group of stakeholders, such as shareholders. Although this perspective applies an equal responsibility across all the firm's stakeholders, when CSR advocates envision what such constraints might look like in reality, they often focus disproportionately on the role of the government. Of course, there is good reason for this as the government has demonstrated on many occasions the value that can be obtained for society by seeking to curb the strongest self-interest impulses of for-profit firms:

> Before the Clean Air Act was passed in 1970 many Americans led shorter, sicker lives because of pollution. White-collar workers in Gary, Indiana, a steel town, often went to work with an extra shirt because the first one looked too dirty by midday. Between 1980 and 2012 total emissions of six common air pollutants in America dropped by 67 percent, according to the Environmental Protection Agency (EPA). This happened even as the country's population grew by 38 percent and Americans consumed 27 percent more energy.[16]

In reality, however, the balance between government oversight and free enterprise is a fine line that governments often cross, with less-than-optimal outcomes. The guiding principle should be to protect the freedom to innovate and avoid central planning, while curbing the greatest excesses of capitalism that can result in counter-productive outcomes for the majority:[17]

> To reconcile the goals of freedom and economic progress, which are paramount in the laissez-faire philosophy, with the goals of

stability, security, justice, and personality development, which are emphasized in modern humanitarian philosophy.[18]

It is this interplay that forms the foundation of modern market capitalism that, via for-profit firms, is the superior structure for combining scarce and valuable resources in ways that promote overall value. In other words, market forces generate better solutions than those arrived at through market distortions, such as coercion (e.g., government regulations) or price controls (e.g., subsidies or quotas). The problem with such distortions is that, however well-intentioned, they have a habit of producing unintended consequences.

Unintended Consequences

When market forces are subverted with ulterior goals, unintended consequences are common. At the extreme, the actual consequences achieve the opposite of those that were intended. An example of this might be if an increase in the minimum wage (designed to protect low-wage earners) were to result in a reduction in overall jobs (reducing the number of low-wage jobs available). This effect is based on the assumption that:

> In a competitive market anything that artificially raises the price of labour will curb demand for it, and the first to lose their jobs will be the least skilled—the people intervention is supposed to help. . . . [T]opping up the incomes of the working poor with public subsidies [is] a far more sensible means of alleviating poverty.[19]

Economists refer to this phenomenon of unintended consequences as *Jevon's paradox*, "named after a 19th-century British economist who observed that while the steam engine extracted energy more efficiently from coal, it also stimulated so much economic growth that coal consumption increased."[20] A modern update of this example is the unforeseen consequences of energy efficiency, particularly in consumer products, such as appliances or cars. While these innovations undoubtedly use energy more efficiently than the technologies they were designed to replace, there is often a compelling argument that the net energy consumed as a result of their purchase is zero (i.e., unchanged) or even positive (i.e., an overall increase):

> The problem is known as the energy rebound effect. While there's no doubt that fuel-efficient cars burn less gasoline per mile, the lower cost at the pump tends to encourage extra driving. There's also an indirect rebound effect as drivers use the money they save on gasoline to buy other things that produce greenhouse emissions, like new electronic gadgets or vacation trips on fuel-burning planes.[21]

A related term for this ability to convince ourselves that the best way to solve our excessive resource depletion of the Earth is through further consumption is "The Prius Fallacy."[22] By substituting one (possibly) greener product for another, we kill two birds with one stone—we satisfy both our psychological and material needs. What we fail to realize, however, is that, even as we innovate, rather than reducing our environmental impact, the unintended consequence is exactly the opposite. While generally ignored by environmentalists today, there are important policy implications from this work:

> If your immediate goal is to reduce greenhouse emissions, then it seems risky to count on reaching it by improving energy efficiency. To economists worried about rebound effects, it makes more sense to look for new carbon-free sources of energy, or to impose a direct penalty for emissions, like a tax on energy generated from fossil fuels. Whereas people respond to more fuel-efficient cars by driving more and buying other products, they respond to a gasoline tax simply by driving less.[23]

The danger becomes particularly prevalent when artificial economic incentives are added to the consumption equation:

> During the time of British rule in colonial India, in order to free Delhi from a plague of snakes, the City's governor put an incentive scheme in place for their capture by introducing a bounty

on cobra skins. The bounty was quite high as cobras are tricky to catch. And so, instead of the snakes being caught in the city, it became a sound business idea to start farming them. All of a sudden, the number of bounty claims increased disproportionately. The local authority realised what was going on and responded by abandoning the incentive scheme. And as they were no longer profitable, the cobras were released from the farms into the city, exacerbating the original problem.[24]

The key to avoiding unforeseen consequences is to ensure the correct behavior is being incentivized:

> Where governments want to raise revenue without distorting markets, the best approach is to charge businesses a flat fee, like a cab licence. Firms then have an incentive to do as much business as they can. But where governments want to discourage consumption—as with cigarettes and alcohol—they should tax each unit sold.[25]

In the example of cobras in India, the desired outcome was a reduction of the number of snakes in Delhi, but the action that was incentivized was an increase in the number of snakes killed. As demonstrated, these things can result in opposite outcomes in practice. In the case of the minimum wage, the goal is to reduce poverty and income disparity. Although economists disagree on the effects of a minimum wage (some research indicates that small increases have little or no effect on job creation), it is possible that in some cases an increase would result in existing employees being fired (because the employer can no longer afford to employ them) or a reduction in the number of new hires (because the cost limits a planned expansion), hence vastly worsening the economic situation for these individuals:

> In flexible economies a low minimum wage seems to have little, if any, depressing effect on employment. America's federal minimum wage, at 38 percent of median income, is one of the rich world's lowest. Some studies find no harm to employment from federal or state minimum wages, others see a small one, but none finds any

serious damage. . . . High minimum wages, however, particularly in rigid labour markets do appear to hit employment. France has the rich world's highest wage floor, at more than 60 percent of the median for adults and a far bigger fraction of the typical wage for the young. This helps explain why France also has shockingly high rates of youth unemployment: 26 percent for 15- to 24-year olds.[26]

The issue of unintended consequences is one of the most important issues for the CSR community to address, particularly in relation to sustainability. When we attempt to subvert centuries of economic development, substituting altruistic motivation for economic incentives, we should tread carefully. Whether it is government subsidies or tax breaks for a particular kind of alternative energy, or a new technical innovation that interacts with some other factor (or is applied inappropriately), the result is often an unexpected outcome that can detract from, rather than promote, overall value. That is not to say that government intervention is necessarily unwarranted or unhelpful. In fact, in terms of shaping the rules of the game to ensure a level playing field and enforcing existing regulations, the government is an essential stakeholder of the firm—what David Sainsbury in his manifesto for progressive capitalism refers to as an enabling state, with responsibilities to support, rather than direct, markets:

> Market institutions are human artefacts created, in all their varieties beyond the most simple, by the state and, ultimately, they all need to be justified by their contribution to the well-being of society and to be perpetually open to reform.[27]

As a general rule, the more heavy-handed or misguided the intervention, the less likely it is to generate an optimal solution. There is still much that we do not understand about the social and economic forces that drive human behavior and generate societal-level outcomes. By definition, we can only base future projections on past experience and are constrained when we do so. When we propose solutions, we envisage the benefits and fail (or are unable) to fully understand all the risks. That does not mean that change should not be implemented, but it does imply we should be humble in attempts to temper these highly complex economic forces that have evolved over centuries. As Adam Smith illustrated in *The Wealth of Nations*:

> The woollen coat, for example, which covers the day-labourer, as coarse and rough as it may appear, is the produce of the joint labour of a multitude of workmen. The shepherd, the sorter of the wool, the wool-comber or carder, the dyer, the scribbler, the spinner, the weaver, the fuller, the dresser, with many others, must all join their different arts in order to complete even this homely production. . . . Let us consider only what a variety of labour is requisite in order to form that very simple machine, the shears with which the shepherd clips the wool. The miner, the builder of the furnace for smelting the ore, the feller of the timber, the burner of the charcoal to be made use of in the smelting-house, the brick-maker, the brick-layer, the workmen who attend the furnace, the mill-wright, the forger, the smith. . . . Without the assistance and co-operation of many thousands, the very meanest person in a civilized country could not be provided, even according to what we very falsely imagine, the easy and simple manner in which he is commonly accommodated.[28]

As Smith insightfully demonstrates, it is the effect of thousands of individuals, each pursuing their individual interests, that collectively ensure the laborer's coat is made in a way that meets the laborer's needs. Most important for CSR advocates is that this pursuit of self-interest is not a process devoid of values. On the contrary, as Adam Gopnik explains in his summary of Adam Smith's work, contrary to popular perceptions, a framework of guiding values is inherently embedded in the application of market forces:

> Where can you find a sympathetic community, people working in uncanny harmony, each aware of the desires of the other and responding to them with grace and reciprocal charm? Forget the shepherds in Arcadia. Ignore the poets in Parnassus. Visit a mall. For Smith the plain-seeing Scot, the market may not be the most

elegant instance of human sympathy, but it's the most insistent: everybody has skin in the game. . . . That's what keeps the mob from rushing the Victoria's Secret and stealing knives from the Hoffritz and looting the Gap. Shopping, which for the church moralist is a straight path to sin, is for Smith a shortcut to sympathy. Money is the surest medium of exchange.[29]

The phenomenon of *Jevons paradox* demonstrates that good intentions that seek to subvert market forces and established market practices can result in counterproductive outcomes. Markets are far from perfect and can distort behavior. As such, the conflicting stakeholder interests described in Principle 4 demonstrate the value in building checks and balances that can curb the market's worst excesses. The ideal would be to design more intelligent curbs that avoid unforeseen consequences by accounting for what we know of the imperfections involved in implementing market ideology—that is, accounting for human behavior.

Behavioral Economics

In 2002, the psychologist Daniel Kahneman won the Nobel Prize for Economics for his work on the cognitive biases of humans. In his 2011 book, *Thinking, Fast and Slow*,[30] he notes that the human brain works with two systems—one system helps make decisions rapidly based on emotion (fast thinking), while a second system helps make decisions more deliberately (slow thinking), but often rationalizes the choices generated by the first system. The combination creates a contrast between the rational, agentic decision makers that we think we are and the emotional, impulsive decision makers that the evidence suggests we are more often:

> Although humans are not irrational, they often need help to make more accurate judgments and better decisions, and in some cases policies and institutions can provide that help. . . . The assumption that agents are rational provides the intellectual foundation for the libertarian approach to public policy: do not interfere with the individual's right to choose, unless the choices harm others. . . . For behavioral economists, however, freedom has a cost, which is

borne by individuals who make bad choices, and by a society that feels obligated to help them.[31]

Many of these ideas, which integrate insights from economics and psychology (social and cognitive), form the foundation of what today is known as behavioral (or nudge)[32] economics. The advantage of behavioral economics is that it works with what we know of the imperfections of human nature to curb the raw excesses of market forces, yet preserves the illusion of choice that markets enable and is an essential component of an open society:

> Behavioural economists have found that all sorts of psychological or neurological biases cause people to make choices that seem contrary to their best interests. The idea of nudging is based on research that shows it is possible to steer people toward better decisions by presenting choices in different ways.[33]

If there was wider use of behavioral economics in policy making, it is argued, we would be able to nudge individuals to make decisions that better serve their own and society's interests. When deployed intelligently, the results can be powerful:

> In one trial, a letter sent to non-payers of vehicle taxes was changed to use plainer English, along the line of "pay your tax or lose your car." In some cases the letter was further personalised by including a photo of the car in question. The rewritten letter alone doubled the number of people paying the tax; the rewrite with the photo tripled it. . . . A study into the teaching of technical drawing in French schools found that if the subject was called "geometry" boys did better, but if it was called "drawing" girls did equally well or better. Teachers are now being trained to use the appropriate term.[34]

Nudge economics demonstrates the value of an accurate, grounded understanding of human behavior—that is, explaining behavior in terms of empirical examination rather than ideological assumptions. The results when implemented demonstrate how human action can be shaped dramatically by applying this knowledge to public policy (and, by extension, to market interactions):

> When you renew your driver's license, you have a chance to enroll in an organ donation program. In countries like Germany and the U.S., you have to check a box if you want to opt in. Roughly 14 percent of people do. But behavioral scientists have discovered that how you set the defaults is really important. So in other countries, like Poland or France, you have to check a box if you want to opt out. In these countries, more than 90 percent of people participate.[35]

It is fascinating how relatively simple incentive structures can be used to nudge people in the direction of better choices and greater societal value in various settings. One more example presents the dramatic shifts in eating behavior achieved through subtle changes to the layout of a school cafeteria:

> A smarter lunchroom wouldn't be draconian. Rather, it would nudge students toward making better choices on their own by changing the way their options are presented. One school we have observed in upstate New York, for instance, tripled the number of salads students bought simply by moving the salad bar away from the wall and placing it in front of the cash registers.[36]

In considering the value of behavioral economics for *strategic CSR*, it is important to think through two considerations. On the one hand, what rights do consumers have to purchase resource intensive products, even if we assume that the full costs associated with producing that product (i.e., all externalities) are incorporated into its purchase price? Should we have the right to destroy the environment if that is the result of the decisions we make (consciously or unconsciously)? On the other hand, what role should the government play in micromanaging our lives, given the blunt tools it uses to decide where to draw the lines, as well as the biased and corrupt process by which it does it (due to the role of money in determining which lines at which times)? The debate between the value of a strong, benevolent government that can shape a progressive society (in theory) and the inefficiency and unintended outcomes associated with top-down directives (in reality), is extremely difficult to resolve:

> Milton Friedman didn't need behavioral economics to know that each of us typically spends our own money on ourselves more wisely than a stranger spends other people's money on us.[37]

My first instinct was to agree. After all, government has certainly demonstrated an inability to shape outcomes better than (or even as well as) markets. On second thought, however, it is also clear that we are often incapable of making good decisions when left to our own intuition. Because human decisions are driven by our inherent and persistent fallibilities—bounded rationality, innate biases, emotional impulses, and cognitive constraints—we often make short-term decisions that do not serve our own long-term interests. This happens even when we are trying to be rational—there are good reasons, for example, why most people fail to save sufficient money for their retirement.

Given that we are living in a system designed and operated by humans, where is the balance between government oversight and individual enterprise? As an integral component of *strategic CSR*, behavioral economics helps push the debate in a helpful direction. Cass Sunstein, who wrote *Nudge* with Richard Thaler, for example, draws on human frailties, such as "'framing effects' (our interpretation of facts is affected by how they are presented to us) and 'status-quo bias' (we prefer the status quo, simply because it is the status quo, over potential alternatives) to promote what he calls 'libertarian paternalism:'"[38]

> Government, he thinks, should change behavior using "nudges" instead of commands. Regulations can tap into people's psychological quirks and prompt them to choose "better" behaviors— while still leaving them free in many circumstances to act differently. Cigarette packages with grisly images of cancer-ridden lungs are an effort to nudge—rather than command—people not to smoke.[39]

It is important to tread carefully here. There is a reason why the market economy has proved so resilient—it draws on core human values and desires and applies them in a way that optimizes outcomes. And, if anything, we are inertial—captive to patterns and biases that are deeply ingrained in all of us. As Bill Frederick reminds us:

> What we are today is, to a very large extent, a function of what we were yesterday. . . this means [for business practitioners] that there is not likely to be any escape from the very powerful motive of private gain and profit, which is often at variance with social interest.[40]

In other words, it is important to work within the constraints of human nature as it is, rather than as we would wish it to be. Behavioral economics does this by incorporating aspects of social and cognitive psychology into economic models that otherwise make unrealistic assumptions about human behavior. As the noted economist, N. Gregory Mankiw, admits:

> We economists often have only a basic understanding of how most policies work. The economy is complex and economic science is still a primitive body of knowledge. Because unintended consequences are the norm, what seems like a utility-maximizing policy can often backfire. . . . In some ways, economics is like medicine two centuries ago. If you were ill at the beginning of the 19th century, a physician was your best bet, but his knowledge was so rudimentary that his remedies could easily make things worse rather than better. And so it is with economics today.[41]

Behavioral economics incorporates the biases and prejudices that inform our decisions into policies that encourage optimal social outcomes, while still retaining the illusion of choice. As such, it is a valuable consideration in the debate between government oversight and unrestricted market forces and, therefore, is an important part of *strategic CSR*.

Summary

Principle 5 states that *Market-based solutions are optimal.* It argues that, while markets are far from perfect, they are the most efficient means we have of allocating scarce and valuable resources via the for-profit firms that populate them. More importantly, the evidence suggests that, when we seek to subvert these highly developed forces, however well-intentioned, the result is often an unintended consequence. One way to curb the raw excesses of market forces, yet preserve the illusion of choice that markets enable, is the wider use of behavioral economics in order to nudge individuals to make decisions that better serve their own and society's interests.

Profit = Economic Value + Social Value

In brief: A firm's profit represents the ability to sell a good or service at a higher price than what it costs to produce. Production and consumption, however, are more than merely technical decisions; they encapsulate the total value (economic and social) that is added by the firm.

A significant reason for the supremacy of market forces in delivering value, as discussed in Principle 5, is the pivotal role played by profit:

> The existence of a profit is an indication *prima facie* that the business has succeeded in producing something which consumers want and value. . . . [A] business that fails to make an adequate profit is a house of cards. It cannot grow or provide more jobs or pay higher wages. In the long run, it cannot even survive. It offers no stability or security or opportunity for its workers and investors. It cannot meet its broader obligations to society. It is a failure from all points of view.[1]

I would amend that quote only to replace the narrow stakeholder group, *consumers*, with the much broader concept of *society*. If a society (the collective group of all stakeholders) permits a firm to continue operations, then it is essentially acknowledging that the organization adds value—that society is better off than if the organization did not exist. At present, the best means we have of measuring that value is the profit the firm generates. This statement is core to the idea of *strategic CSR*, but exists in contrast to the way that profit is usually discussed within the CSR community—as a narrow measure of economic value and something that can detract from social value. This representation of *economic value* and *social value* as independent constructs demonstrates a fundamental misunderstanding of what profit represents. In reality, economic value and social value are highly correlated assets.

Economic Value + Social Value

The profit motive is closely linked in business to the price mechanism, which is an assessment of the cost of bringing a product or service to market, plus a margin that provides sufficient incentive for the business to operate. In the marketplace, *price* is the best way we have developed to measure the value added in an exchange. In terms of firm performance, a profit or loss is the aggregated outcome of multiple production and consumption decisions. These decisions are arrived at through individual evaluations of cost and benefit along many, many dimensions, and expressed in the consumer's willingness to pay the price that is being charged. If the value I obtain from a product exceeds the costs involved in earning sufficient money to pay the price, then I should be willing to buy it. In other words, when I buy a product, I am signaling to the firm that I value that product. When this transaction is repeated on a society-wide basis, this signal amounts to a social sanction of the underlying business:

> When businessmen [sic] follow the profit motive they are merely following social valuations as expressed in the prices at which they can sell their products and the prices at which they can buy productive services, materials, supplies, and their other requirements. . . . When the businessman follows this signal, he is following not only his own interest but that of society as well. . . . The practical and the democratic thing for him to do is to rely primarily on profit as his guide in deciding his business actions.[2]

Conceptually, therefore, while it can be helpful to think of economic value and social value as separate constructs; in reality, they are not independent. On the contrary, they are highly correlated and are infused in the firm's decisions regarding production (e.g., Do we pollute the local river, or not? Do we hire at the minimum wage or a living wage?) and the consumer's decisions regarding consumption (e.g., Do I buy from the firm that produces domestically or the one that outsources? Do I pay the premium associated with a more environmentally-friendly product or purchase the cheaper, disposable product?). All of these production and consumption decisions contain value-laden consequences that, ultimately, determine the economic success of the firm:

> 200 year's worth of work in economics and finance indicate that social welfare is maximized when all firms in an economy maximize total firm value. The intuition behind this criterion is simply that (social) value is created when a firm produces an output or set of outputs that are valued by its customers at more than the value of the inputs it consumes (as valued by their suppliers) in such production. Firm value is simply the long-term market value of this stream of benefits.[3]

Similarly, we know from a significant body of research in fields such as strategy and marketing that, when I buy a product, I am not just purchasing something that will fulfill a technical function—I am buying something that makes me happy, that conveys my status, that boosts my self-esteem, and, yes, something that is socially responsible (depending on the values I hold and the criteria I prioritize in my purchase decisions). This is something that we all know intuitively to be true. It is why car companies like BMW, Mercedes, and Audi exist—they provide a product that does much more for the consumer than transport them from point A to point B.

In addition to this private, nontechnical value that is built into the price the consumer pays for a good, there is also a component that relates to the level of public value generated. If I buy a Toyota Prius, for example, I pay a price premium over similar, nonhybrid cars because of the superior technology built into the Prius' engine. While I get a private benefit from this purchase in that I can now demonstrate to everyone how environmentally conscious I am, there is also a significant public benefit in the reduced pollution that my car emits. In this, the price premium I am paying represents a subsidy to society in that I am covering the cost of improving the air quality—a positive externality from which everyone benefits, but is built into the price that I pay. More specifically, by providing this product that reduces environmental pollution, is Toyota engaged in solving an economic problem (the demand for cars) or a social problem (the need to transport people in a way that minimizes damage to the environment)?

Management researchers talk about the need for "compassion in organizations" that allows them also to "focus on social problems and social welfare concerns"[4] as if economic problems and social problems are separate entities. Again, a simple thought experiment highlights the overly simplistic nature of this forced dichotomy. Is feeding people a social problem or an economic problem? Of course, there are hundreds of for-profit food manufacturers (not to mention the hundreds of thousands of restaurants) that produce food and distribute it widely (and efficiently) to whole populations of people. What about clothing people—a social problem or an economic problem? A visit to the mall will quickly reveal how efficiently for-profit firms have essentially eradicated the supply of clothes as a challenge for all but the most deprived societies. Or, what about providing Internet access to every household in the country—economic or social? Certainly, you could make an argument that, today, a family is essentially excluded from many aspects of society if it cannot get online ("what many people consider as basic a utility as water and electricity");[5] yet, Internet provision in most developed economies is the sole responsibility of the private sector (as it is for the food and apparel industries).

So, how is it that for-profit firms are not already intricately involved in addressing social problems? In fact, you could argue that essentially every company uses economic means to solve social problems. Now, you may challenge the business models of some of these firms, or the quality of the final product they produce, but I believe there is no way that anyone can say these for-profit firms are not involved in addressing complex problems that have intertwined economic and social (and ethical and moral) components. In essence, there are no economic problems or social problems; there are just problems that have both social and economic consequences.

As the earlier examples indicate, much of what is referred to as social value (the value that is derived above and beyond the functional purpose of a product or service) is captured in a willingness among consumers to part with their disposable income. Given that, for most of us, our disposable income is a scarce resource, how we decide to spend it reflects our values in action. That is not to say that market forces are perfect. Unfortunately, 100 percent of social value is not captured in the price charged and the profit earned. Negative externalities are a good example of how imperfect the market can be (e.g., pollution during manufacturing that goes undetected, or the pollution involved during consumption that is not accounted for in the product's price). Human beings' tendency to favor short-term gratification over longer-term investments (which explains why most people fail to save sufficient funds for their retirement) is another example of how the private profits that are generated immediately as a result of our consumption decisions do not reflect perfectly the public costs incurred by society at some later date:

> The profit motive can be objected to legitimately when the quest for profits results in restrictive monopoly, exploitation, fraud, misrepresentation, political bribery, waste of nature resources, economic insecurity, etc. It is the *abuse* of the profit motive, not the motive itself, that comes under criticism.[6]

In other words, given what we know, monetary value is the best way we have of capturing overall value creation. The price of a product and the profit of a firm incorporate a significant amount of all aspects of value (economic, social, moral, etc.) that is encapsulated in market transactions. While the correlation among these different measures of value is high, however, it is not perfect. As such, *strategic CSR* exists to redefine our understanding of economic exchanges in order to minimize the gap between different measures of value. One example of this is to ensure that firms internalize the complete costs of production and consumption in the price that is charged for the finished good. This issue will be discussed in detail in Principle 7. Before we turn to that discussion, however, it is necessary to complete our consideration of the role played by profit in overall value creation.

Profit Optimization

In the process of delivering value to its broad range of stakeholders, it is essential that the firm generates a profit. Profit generation is, therefore, also central to the concept of *strategic CSR*. Rather than challenge what the firm does (make money), however, *strategic CSR* is focused more specifically on how the firm does it (the hundreds and thousands of operational decisions made every day). In the process, one of the goals of *strategic CSR* is to change the debate around the role of the for-profit firm in society. By challenging taken-for-granted assumptions about business and the value it delivers, the potential for reform that helps build a more sustainable economic system becomes possible. One of the taken-for-granted assumptions that must be challenged is the idea that firms pursue policies and practices that result in *profit maximization*. First, this concept is not possible; second, it is unhelpful.

First, the idea of profit maximization is something that is impossible to prove as a firm can never know whether the profit generated was in fact maximized or what effect making an alternative decision would have had instead:

> A simple statement that managers try to maximize corporate profits, as is frequently assumed in economic theory, is almost meaningless. The concept of profit is a highly tenuous one in that it involves the valuation of assets, the allocation of joint costs, the treatment of developmental expenses, and a host of similar problems for which there are no easy or definite solutions. The idea of profit maximization raises the troublesome question of the time period over which profits are to be maximized, and it is difficult for either managers or observers to calculate the effect on profits of given actions which may affect the business indefinitely in the future. Obviously, businessmen [sic] are often deterred by custom and by ethical principle from exacting the highest possible profit. The businessman may forgo profits to avoid the demands of organized labor, or public regulation, or entry of new firms. Businessmen often show greater interest in business volume and business expansion than they do in profits. . . . It may be more realistic to describe the quest for profit as a seeking for "satisfactory profits" rather than maximum profits ("satisfactory" defined in relation to the profit experience of other firms).[7]

Second, the idea of profit maximization is unhelpful. It is a fallacy and, as such, distorts expectations and decision making within the firm. The only way that we can know if a particular set of decisions *maximized* profits for the firm is to rerun the time period, under the exact internal and external conditions, investigating all the different possible combinations of decision outcomes, one at a time. Given that there is no control group[8] for any firm (the only option is to choose a similar competitor, which, however similar, will have many differences to the focal firm), there is no way to know whether the current profits are any higher or lower than if different decisions had been made. As such, the decision matrix that will guide the firm comes down to a debate among different philosophies (e.g., Do you believe paying a minimum wage to employees will generate larger profits than paying a living wage?). Any firm or individual executive that claims his or her set of decisions will maximize profits for the firm is, therefore, being disingenuous at best; most likely, he or she does not fully understand the nature of the statement and certainly cannot in any way prove the claim. As Robert Skidelsky reminds us:

> Economics is luxuriant with fallacies, because it is not a natural science like physics or chemistry. Propositions in economics are rarely absolutely true or false. What is true in some circumstances may be false in others. Above all, the truth of many propositions depends on people's expectations.[9]

As a result of being both impossible to achieve and unhelpful because it distorts decision making, rather than profit *maximization*, a more valuable focus for firms to adopt is the goal of profit *optimization*. Although equally impossible to prove definitively, profit optimization (rather than maximization) is a flexible goal that more closely approximates the subjective nature of the decision-making process—different people will use different sets of values to determine what they consider to be *optimal*. In other words, while the idea of a *maximum* suggests an absolute point (a definitive maximum amount), an *optimum* suggests a more relative state of existence. What is optimal for me, may not be optimal for you, but you cannot say the values by which I determine my optimum are *wrong*—just that they differ from the values you use to determine your optimum.

As such, this rhetorical shift helps encourage a balance between short-, medium-, and long-term decisions that create value across the firm's broad range of stakeholders.

Production Value and Consumption Value

As the earlier discussion indicates, while defining social value and economic value and understanding how they relate to each other appears superficially straightforward, it is highly complex in reality. Beyond a conceptual discussion, it is also useful to think through the challenges of drawing this distinction in practice. For example: Do employees' wages relate to economic value (a cost of production) or social value (a determinant of income inequality)? Similarly, is the level of pollution related to economic value (an output of production) or social value (a blight that is borne by society)? In both cases, you might answer both and, of course, you would be correct. In reality, there is no *social value* and no *economic value*; there is only *value* that is distributed among all stakeholders. As such, any attempt to present these highly complex and complementary concepts as independent demonstrates a fundamental misunderstanding of the roles firms play in society, but also of the ability of profit to capture what people mean when they talk about social value.

Given these complexities, an alternative conceptualization is to think of the value added by a firm during production and the value added by a product or service during consumption. At either stage, the assessment of the value added would be either neutral, net positive, or net negative. In this alternative conceptualization, employees' wages would contribute to the total value added during production, as would any pollution emitted during manufacturing, while pollution emitted during consumption (e.g., driving a car, the e-waste created by a discarded phone, TV, or mp3 player) would be accounted for as part of the value added (or subtracted) during consumption. The net effect, in theory, would define our collective quality of life, which would in turn help determine necessary reforms:

> Our standard of living . . . consists of two parts: that which derives from the conditions under which production is carried on and that which derives from the goods and services resulting from that

production. An improvement in the conditions of production—resulting in a better working environment of better functioning of the economy—may frequently be entirely justified even if achieved at a sacrifice in output of final goods and services.[10]

The challenge we face as a society, therefore, is to strike a balance between the part of our standard of living that is formed from the production of goods and services, and the part of our standard of living that is formed from the consumption of goods and services. The production component includes incorporating costs that firms currently seek to externalize (such as the pollution emitted during manufacturing), while the consumption component includes incorporating costs that society currently seeks to avoid (such as the pollution emitted during consumption, e.g., driving a car, and recycling, e.g., waste). If a marginal dollar spent on production yields greater returns than the same dollar spent on consumption, it is in our collective best interests to spend the dollar on improving aspects of production (and vice-versa).

In this sense, understanding the true nature of what profit represents is conceptually important, but helpful only up to a point. If we accept that long-term profit is a good (if imperfect) measure of total value added, we must also recognize that it is just that—a measure of performance that still does not help us understand how the firm should add that value:

> Defining what it means to score a goal in football or soccer, for example, tells the players nothing about how to win the game. It just tells them how the score will be kept. That is the role of value maximization in organizational life.[11]

In other words, profit is the outcome of a highly complex process that, more accurately, determines whether the firm is being socially responsible. As such, understanding how firms can balance the pursuit of profit and the need to satisfy a broad range of stakeholder interests (how they should achieve their profit) is essential. This is the purpose of *strategic CSR*, which is a detailed extension of what has been referred to elsewhere as "enlightened stakeholder theory."[12]

Summary

Principle 6 states that *Profit = economic value + social value*. It argues that conceptualizing economic and social value as independent constructs demonstrates a fundamental misunderstanding of what profit represents. Although imperfect, profit is the best measure we have of capturing the total value added by a specific company and product during production and consumption. Rather than asking firms to focus on *profit maximization* (which is both impossible to prove and unhelpful because it distorts decision making), however, the goal of *profit optimization* better reflects the value judgments that are made every day as firms balance competing stakeholder interests. Even better, understanding the extent of value added in terms of the separate processes associated with the production and consumption of products and services provides a mechanism by which society can more easily identify those behaviors that detract from, rather than add to, overall value.

PRINCIPLE 7

The *Free* Market Is an Illusion

In brief: The free market is not *free*. It encourages firms to externalize costs that are then borne by society rather than consumers; it is rife with subsidies and quotas that favor some firms and industries over others. The result is an economic system that is distorted and, as a result, unsustainable.

As demonstrated by Principle 6, although economic value and social value are highly correlated, the relationship is not perfect. In other words, not all of the potential value that society could possibly gain from a business transaction is captured in the profit generated by the firm. The reason for this is that our current economic model is distorted. Essential to building on Principle 6, therefore, is the need to address the structural characteristics that embed barriers to free exchange throughout the economy:

> Industrial policy . . . raises costs for consumers and puts more efficient foreign firms at a disadvantage. The Peterson Institute reckons local-content requirements cost the world $93 billion in lost trade in 2010.[1]

In terms of protectionist policies, the barriers to trade are numerous and, because they are often designed to appease local political constituencies, can appear absurd from afar. America, for example, "tacks a 127 percent tariff on to Chinese paper clips," while "Japan puts a 778 percent tariff on rice,"[2] and, worldwide, $500 billion is spent by governments on energy subsidies, "the equivalent of four times all official foreign aid."[3] For these reasons (and many more—quotas, tax breaks, bailouts, export rebates, etc.), markets are far from freely competitive. Failed oversight and misaligned incentives, in the form of externalities, allow otherwise uncompetitive businesses and harmful products to remain viable, while active intervention, usually by the government, undermines innovation and free enterprise. Overall, the wide variety of market distortions generate an economic system that is less efficient, less competitive, and less sustainable than it otherwise would be.[4]

Free Markets

As currently constituted, "markets fail to price the true costs of goods."[5] The reason for this is that the markets we have created are riddled with inefficiencies (what politicians call subsidies, tax breaks, legal loopholes, etc.). These inefficiencies introduce costs into the system and skew incentives that, together, sustain uncompetitive companies and erect barriers to more competitive alternatives. As such, we need to reform our market system.

The goal should be to work toward a model in which all inefficiencies are eradicated and all costs are included in the price that is charged for each product and service. An economy where externalities are internalized and embedded within a moral framework moves us closer to the economy Adam Smith envisioned and wrote about in his classic treatise *The Theory of Moral Sentiments*[6]—truly free markets filled with values-based businesses and vigilant stakeholders. Instead, we have a very different reality:

> Corporate welfare [by government] is the offer of special favors—cash grants, loans, guarantees, bailouts and special tax breaks—to specific industries or firms. . . . [estimated in the U.S. to be] $92 billion for fiscal 2006, which is more than the U.S. government spends on homeland security. That annual cost may have doubled to $200 billion in this new era of industry bailouts and subsidies. According to the House Budget Committee, the 2009 stimulus bill alone contained more than $80 billion in "clean energy" subsidies, and tens of billions more went for the auto bailout and cash for clunkers, as well as aid for the mortgage industry through programs to refinance or buy up toxic loans.[7]

Politicians on both the left and the right tend to favor government intervention when it is in support of a cause in which they believe (e.g., subsidies for solar power on the left, tax breaks for oil firms on the right), but at least the left admits that it favors government intervention. Right-wing ideology, in contrast, preaches free market ideas, but then implements heavily subsidized intervention in contravention of that ideology. What the prior quote about corporate welfare does not include, therefore, is the recognition that subsidies and quotas are only one component of the inefficient system of corporate support that we have created in the West. A good example of these distortions occur in the energy market:

> Economics 101 tells us that an industry imposing large costs on third parties should be required to "internalize" those costs. . . . [Energy extraction by] Fracking might still be worth doing given those costs. But no industry should be held harmless from its impacts on the environment and the nation's infrastructure. Yet what the industry and its defenders demand is, of course, precisely that it be let off the hook for the damage it causes. Why? Because we need that energy![8]

In a similar way, a significant cost associated with nuclear energy is absorbed by government when it takes responsibility for waste containment. While there is a significant national security interest in doing so, the effect is to externalize the true cost of nuclear power generation. It is the combination of reduced government intervention (i.e., the removal of subsidies, quotas, tax breaks, etc.) *plus* the internalization of all externalities in pricing that allows a truly free market to emerge. One without the other is not *free*; at present, we have neither:

> So it's worth pointing out that special treatment for fracking makes a mockery of free-market principles. Pro-fracking politicians claim to be against subsidies, yet letting an industry impose costs without paying compensation is in effect a huge subsidy. They say they oppose having the government "pick winners," yet they demand special treatment for this industry precisely because they claim it will be a winner.[9]

In this light, a government tax on carbon is simply a means of accounting for the full environmental costs of oil or gas extraction, processing, and consumption. In other words, it is a means of creating the conditions for a *free* market. Once the level-playing field has been created (with more accurate prices for all forms of energy—traditional and alternative), then the market will determine which energy sources should drive our future economies. Ultimately:

> Markets are truly free only when everyone pays the full price for his or her actions. Anything else is socialism. . . . Our future will largely be determined by our ability to admit the need to end planetary socialism. That's the most fundamental of economics lessons and one any serious environmentalist ought to heed.[10]

Externalities

The perspective of most economic theory is that, over the long run, prices are formed by the market in response to demand and supply and are outside the control of individual firms. In other words, in the long run, firms can only charge what market forces will allow them to charge. Any higher and the firm will lose business to its competitors; any lower and the firm will, at a minimum, leave money on the table and, more likely, will operate at a loss.

The problem with this theory is twofold: First, many of the assumptions that accompany it (free and open competition, perfect information, free mobility and choice of sellers and buyers, etc.) are rarely, if ever, present; and second, that most business occurs in the short run—as Keynes noted, "In the long run we are all dead."[11] As a result, markets are imperfect. In essence, prices do not capture all costs associated with production and consumption. Given the opportunity, firms will externalize costs, allowing others (society, broadly speaking) to incur them. Thus, firms are not directly responsible for building roads, although they benefit greatly from using them to transport goods; they also do not pay for a country's education system, although they benefit greatly from employing an educated workforce, and so on. These costs are all what economists refer to as an *externality*, which the *Oxford English Dictionary* defines as:

> A side-effect or consequence (of an industrial or commercial activity) which affects other parties without this being reflected

in the cost of the goods or services involved; a social cost or benefit.[12]

An *externality* is a cost (or benefit) that is incurred, but not paid for, either by the firm (during production) or the purchaser (during consumption):

> Over the past century, companies have been rewarded financially for maximizing externalities in order to minimize costs. . . . Not until we more broadly "price in" the external costs of investment decision across all sectors will we have a sustainable economy and society.[13]

While it takes 500 to 2,000 liters of water to produce the 4 oz. of ginned cotton necessary to make a cotton t-shirt, for example, the farmer who produced that cotton receives only approximately $0.20 for his or her crop.[14] This is because, in many countries, water is provided free or is heavily subsidized by the state in ways that fail to reflect either the true value of water in the production process, or the cost of replenishing stocks so that others may have a guaranteed supply in the future. Clearly, this is less than optimal because it distorts the normal interaction of demand and supply to create an artificially low price (and distorted market) for, in this case, t-shirts.

If we are to reconsider fundamentally our economic model, the most important step is to account adequately for externalities in pricing. In other words, the price of a product should not only include the cost of production, but also include the cost of replenishing the raw material and disposing or recycling the waste after consumption. If all firms were forced to incorporate externalities into the price of the finished product or service, many of the cheap items in our disposable economy will become significantly more expensive and businesses would be incentivized to produce sustainable alternatives.

Lifecycle Pricing

A major flaw in economic theory will remain if we continue to allow resources to be treated as though they are infinite. There is only one planet and, as much research has demonstrated, we are already placing significant constraints on the resources at our disposal:

> Some seven billion people are alive today; the United Nations estimates that by the end of the century we could number as many as 15.8 billion. Biologists have calculated that an ideal population—the number at which everyone could live at a first-world level of consumption, without ruining the planet irretrievably—would be 1.5 billion. . . . Each year the world adds the equivalent of another Germany or Egypt; by 2040, China will have more than 100 million 80-year-olds. We add another million people every four and a half days.[15]

Population level, in itself, however, is not necessarily a problem. It is a large population combined with a materialistic lifestyle that places such a strain on resource levels:

> If everyone on Earth lived the lifestyle of a traditional Indian villager, it is arguable that even 12 billion would be a sustainable world population. If everyone lives like an upper-middle-class North American (a status to which much of the world seems to aspire), then even two billion is unsustainable.[16]

There is a cost to extraction, production, and consumption without replenishment.[17] Waste, whether it occurs during production or consumption, is a significant economic and ecological drag on efficiency.[18] Externalities distort markets and underprice products that generate long-term ecological damage. Where resources can be replenished, we need to account for those costs in the prices that are charged to consumers. Where resources cannot be replenished, we need to impose a cost that accounts for the loss to humanity that results from their extraction. As Paul Hawken astutely puts it:

> Without doubt, the single most damaging aspect of the present economic system is that the expense of destroying the earth is largely absent from the prices set in the marketplace.[19]

One idea that has been proposed to solve the problem of externalities by accounting for (internalizing) these *true* costs is *lifecycle pricing*[20] (related to the idea of *Pigovian taxes*).[21] In other words, the price of a product should not only include the cost of production, but also include the costs associated with replenishing the raw materials used and disposing or recycling of the waste after consumption.[22] Attempts to put a price on carbon reflect this process (either through a carbon tax or some form of cap-and-trade), while firms' efforts to measure the carbon footprints of their products[23] provide a possible means of implementation.

The core idea behind lifecycle pricing is to capture all of the impacts of the production process at each step in the supply chain and assign a quantitative value to that step. At the risk of oversimplifying a highly complex process (managing to avoid double-counting is, in itself, extremely challenging); in essence, lifecycle pricing requires a firm to add up the positive and negative costs in the value chain to arrive at a net impact score for each product. This is important because, "If prices reflected all the costs, including ecological costs spread across generations, the world would not face sustainability challenges; at least in theory."[24] The debate surrounding the pricing of "natural capital" (the resources that exist naturally and are exploited by business, often for free—a form of "environmental profit and loss accounting")[25] is central to this task:

> Natural capital is simple. The value of well-functioning natural systems is clearly manifest to all people and companies—in the form of clean air, reliable availability of freshwater and productive topsoil in which to grow food, among other benefits. Yet, the way that finance works—from GDP calculations to corporate accounting—it is as if reliable flows from well-functioning natural systems have no value.[26]

One of the earliest adopters of the concept of environmental profit and loss (EP&L) accounting was Puma. The firm developed and first published an EP&L statement in 2011, in which it concluded its operations had an "impact of €51 million resulting from land use, air pollution and waste along the value chain added to previously announced €94 million for GHG emissions and water consumption."[27] It is an idea that is making progress—according to some reports, up to 200 large firms now account for their use of natural capital to some extent:

> They include Disney and Microsoft, which attach a "shadow price" to their carbon emissions; Colgate Palmolive and EcoLab, which are trying to measure the true cost of water; and Interface, which puts a price on the natural capital consumed by its carpet tiles.[28]

If this process of quantifying the costs incurred at all stages of the value chain (extraction, processing, manufacture, wholesale or retail, purchase or consumption, disposal or recycling), including the transportation and storage between each stage, as well as all other resource inputs (e.g., energy and other materials), and accounting for the costs of dealing with the outputs generated at each stage (such as waste materials and other forms of pollution), firms would have an accurate snapshot of the true costs involved in producing a product.

Perhaps the best example of a firm that has comprehensively attempted to integrate a lifecycle approach throughout all aspects of operations is Interface carpets, whose inspirational founder and CEO, the late Ray Anderson, explained his journey in terms of the seven (+1) faces of *Mount Sustainability*: (1) waste, (2) emissions, (3) energy, (4) materials, (5) transportation, (6) culture, (7) market, and (8) social equity.[29] In Anderson's vision, the peak of the mountain represents *sustainability*, which he defines as "take nothing, do no harm." The natural conclusion of such a *cradle-to-cradle*, closed-loop system throughout a firm's value chain is zero waste. Anderson expanded on his vision of the business logic of sustainability ("Project Zero," to be reached by 2020) at the TED conference in 2009:

> More happiness with less stuff. You know, that would reframe civilization itself and our whole system of economics—if not for our species, then perhaps for the one that succeeds us—the sustainable species, living on a finite earth, ethically, happily, and ecologically in balance with nature and all her natural systems for a thousand generations or ten thousand generations. . . . But, does the Earth have to wait for our extinction as a species . . . I don't think so. At Interface, we really intend to bring this prototypical,

sustainable, zero-footprint industrial company fully into existence by 2020. We can see our way now clear to the top of that mountain and now the challenge is in execution.[30]

It is only by developing industry-wide standards within a lifecycle pricing model that we will move closer to understanding the holistic impact of our current economic system and business practices.[31] We have created an economic system based around convenience and waste—we spend money we do not have, on things we do not want, for purposes that are often unimportant.[32] Even recycling is an insufficient goal within a lifecycle framework. Instead, we need to move toward *upcycling* because "almost all products can be recycled only as low-grade reclaimed basic substances, and the recycling process itself consumes a great deal of energy and labor."[33]

In short, we need to find a way to decrease our unsustainable exploitation of virgin resources. If companies are forced to price finished products accurately, many of the cheap items in our disposable economy will become significantly more expensive and businesses will be incentivized to produce sustainable alternatives. The market remains the most effective means we know of allocating scarce and valuable resources in ways that maximize social outcomes. Rather than subsidizing specific industries, adequately pricing the *true* cost of a product allows for a less distorted competition of ideas in the marketplace that should also generate socially responsible outcomes.

Summary

Principle 7 states that *The* free *market is an illusion*. It argues that, at present, our economic system allows firms to externalize costs (to society) that are then not included in the prices that are charged (to customers). The problem, therefore, is not that the price mechanism does not work; the problem is that all relevant costs are not currently included in the prices that are charged. And, if prices are distorted, the resulting economic exchange will also be distorted. While the production of goods is distorted because the costs of bringing a product to market are lowered, the consumption of those goods is also distorted because the prices charged are similarly lowered. Not only does this create an artificial market for products currently being produced and consumed, but it also creates artificial barriers to entry for more competitive alternatives. The solution lies in *lifecycle pricing*, where all related costs of production and consumption are incorporated into the final prices charged.

Scale Matters; Only Business Can Save the Planet

In brief: The environmental challenge has reached the point where consumer-driven change is insufficient. While for-profit firms were the main cause of the problem, they are also the main hope for a solution. Scale is vital and large firms must do much more if we are to create a sustainable economic system.

When we begin to internalize Principle 7, we begin to understand the scale of the changes that are necessary. This leads to two conclusions: First, we cannot get there via higher levels of consumption—at least, not with our current economic model that equates progress with waste.[1] A more dramatic change is necessary. At the end of his documentary, *An Inconvenient Truth*, Al Gore famously presented a call to action—for viewers to "be part of the solution." Having sketched a vision of a global calamity, however, Gore then implores the audience to go home and "change a light bulb" or "plant a tree":

> That's when it got really depressing. The immense disproportion between the magnitude of the problem Gore had described and the puniness of what he was asking us to do about it was enough to sink your heart.[2]

Second, it is not about the actions of the individual, however worthy, but the actions of the for-profit firm. And, in particular, it is the actions of large corporations that will matter most. Scale is central to any meaningful solution. While much of the focus remains on reusing shopping bags and changing light bulbs, the planet is deteriorating before our eyes. In the United States, 88 cities and counties in California alone have introduced bans on free plastic bags[3] and Walmart sells approximately

100 million compact fluorescent light (CFL) light bulbs every year,[4] yet greenhouse gas emissions keep rising:

> The problem we face is far greater than anything portrayed by the media. . . . recycling aluminum cans in the company cafeteria and ceremonial tree plantings are about as effective as bailing out the *Titanic* with teaspoons.[5]

In the face of political intransigence, only for-profit firms are able to deliver the necessary reforms on the scale and at the speed at which they must occur to avert widespread ecological devastation.

Sustainability

In 1987, *The Brundtland Report* was published. The report, which was named after its main author, Gro Harlem Brundtland (Norwegian Prime Minister and chair of the United Nation's World Commission on Environment and Development) was established to investigate the sustainability of our economic development. As well as concluding that our current system is unsustainable, the committee provided a definition of what a sustainable system would look like:

> Sustainable development is development that meets the needs of the present without compromising the ability of future generations to meet their own needs.[6]

The discussion fostered by the report essentially defined the field of sustainability as concerned primarily with resource utilization (in particular, the unsustainable rate of depletion).[7] As such, today, most people understand *sustainability* to represent issues related to the natural environment.[8] Importantly, however, the report was also prescient in framing the central role of business as both the cause of the problem and also the best hope for a solution by more clearly defining the demands society must make of its for-profit firms:

> The Brundtland Report, which inspired the 1992 Earth Summit in Rio de Janeiro that resulted in the Climate Change Convention and in turn the Kyoto Protocol, acknowledged that many

"of the development paths of the industrialized nations are clearly unsustainable." However, it held fast to its embrace of development toward industrialized nation living standards as part of the solution, not part of the problem. "If large parts of countries of the global South are to avert economic, social, and environmental catastrophes, it is essential that global economic growth be revitalized," the report stated.[9]

In the debate over whether we should pursue sustainability via material sacrifice (i.e., produce and consume less) or technological innovation (i.e., produce and consume more), *The Brundtland Report*, with the supporting legitimacy of the United Nations, came down firmly in favor of progress. This presents a clear paradox between the damage to the environment that has been done so far by the industrial revolution and subsequent economic development, and the potential contribution firms can make to create a more sustainable economic system. The key is to move quickly:

> Though it remains technically possible to keep planetary warming to a tolerable level, only an intensive push over the next 15 years . . . can achieve that goal. . . . "We cannot lose another decade," said Ottmar Edenhofer, a German economist and co-chairman of the [Intergovernmental Panel on Climate Change] . . . "[or] it becomes extremely costly to achieve climate stabilization."[10]

In other words, corporations are central to any discussion about the environment. While greenhouse gas emissions from energy use are an important source of total global emissions, for example, they form only 26 percent of the total, with industry (19 percent), forestry (17 percent), agriculture (14 percent), transport (13 percent), buildings (8 percent), and waste (3 percent) contributing collectively a much higher percentage of the total.[11] There is much work to do, especially given the inherent flaws in our economic system that relies on both waste and materialism.

Waste

Waste is a central component of the economic model that drives the global economy. For the majority of for-profit firms, the more you buy of their products, the better they perform and the faster the economy grows. In other words, excessive consumption and quick turnover are essential. Whether we *need* a product is less important than whether we *want* it. And, if we buy a product, the quicker we throw it away and buy another one, the better for all concerned. Restraint and conservation are not encouraged. When you realize that Starbucks goes through 2.3 billion disposable cups every year,[12] you understand that resolving to bring a reusable cup to the store (even if you get all of your friends to do the same) pales in comparison to the scale of the action required to make a difference.

A huge assumption of this economic model is that the world's resources are infinite. As such, when a company extracts a raw material and converts it into something that consumers want to buy, the consumer pays only for the costs the firm incurred during the extraction and conversion. For the most part, there is no charge associated with the replenishment of the resource (e.g., the cost of losing forever the precious metals used in cell phones that are not recycled) or the environmental costs incurred during consumption (e.g., the pollution emitted when driving a car). In short, our economy is founded on *waste*—the more the company and consumers waste, the higher a country's gross domestic product (GDP), and the *stronger* its economy. A question worth asking is "Are we sinking under the weight of our disposable society?"[13]

> According to the OECD, the average person creates 3.3lb (1.5kg) of rubbish a day in France, 2.7lb in Canada and no more than 2.3lb in Japan. By the OECD's reckoning, the average American produces 4.5lb a day, and more recent accounting puts the figure at over 7lb a day, less than a quarter of which is recycled.[14]

Our consumer-oriented economic model dictates that we trade-in our fully functioning old phone and buy a new model whenever one comes out, without thinking through the consequences of that exchange. The problem is particularly acute in terms of the electronic waste (*e-waste*) that we generate in the process. As electronic consumer goods become obsolete and are discarded, the vast array of toxic metals they contain inflict significant costs onto society. Some of these costs can be quantified, while others are done so less easily:

> A 2010 study found that more than 80 percent of young children in Guiyu, China's biggest e-waste processing zone, were suffering from lead poisoning.[15]

As a result, e-waste stands as a poster child for the ecological consequences of our 21st century consumption-based economic model, which treats all resources as infinite and fails to fully account for the externalities created during the manufacturing processes. According to the Environmental Protection Agency, the problem is immense and will only get worse. Already, in the United States alone:

- 142,000 computers and over 416,000 mobile devices are thrown away every day;
- 3.41 million tons of e-waste is discarded annually;
- only 24.9 percent (by total weight) of e-waste is recycled.[16]

Waste, when approached with a more enlightened attitude, however, can be an asset for the firm and add value, broadly defined. Walmart, whose prior CEO (Lee Scott) in 2005 committed the firm to a goal of creating "zero waste,"[17] presents an excellent case-study of what this can look like in practice. Ever since, Walmart has been committed to greatly reducing the waste packaging that is processed through its stores:

> Our packaging team, for example, worked with our packaging supplier to reduce excessive packaging on some of our private-label Kid Connection toy products. By making the packaging just a little bit smaller on one private brand of toys, we will use 497 fewer containers and generate freight savings of more than $2.4 million per year. Additionally, we'll save more than 38-hundred trees and more than a thousand barrels of oil. Again, think about this with Wal-Mart's scale in mind: this represents ONE relatively simple package change on ONE private toy brand.[18]

Importantly, Walmart's commitment also has dramatic ramifications for the tens of thousands of supplier firms with whom Walmart does business every day:

> [Walmart's] decision in 2006 to stock only double concentrate liquid laundry detergent led to the entire US detergent industry shifting to smaller, lighter bottlers by the start of [2008], saving millions of dollars in fuel costs.[19]

Literally, Walmart has the ability to change the world. In addition to appealing to consumers to buy more CFL light bulbs, however, the firm can have its greatest impact on the supply side. In July 2009, for example, the firm announced a commitment:

> To create a global, industry-wide sustainable product index. The ambitious plan . . . aims to establish a sustainability rating system for each item on Wal-Mart's shelves. This will help shoppers understand the social and environmental impact of products. It should also drive innovation among suppliers.[20]

For Walmart, the connection between waste reduction and its overarching business model is clear. Driving waste out of its supply chain will enable the firm to become more efficient through innovation and pass those efficiencies onto its customers in the form of lower prices. The extension of this philosophy to its support of the sustainable product index,[21] ultimately, is designed to enhance consumer education by allowing like-for-like comparison across all consumer products and industries. More importantly, however, it will provide even more data about its supply chain that Walmart can use to drive costs even lower.

Walmart still employs a business model that relies on consumption and disposal. But, in terms of resource utilization, it is heading in the right direction. If Walmart can achieve its stated goal of zero waste, the firm has the potential to revolutionize economic production. A similar enlightened approach to waste is beginning to take hold in the cell phone industry, where there is also a clear business model for doing so:

> Since 2001, Sprint has diverted more than 53m mobile devices from landfills and it offers up to $300 in-store credit for old

devices, including those from other carriers. In 2012, Sprint paid out $100 million in-store credit to customers. . . . Sprint has made it clear that its buyback program isn't just about doing good; the program also has boosted the bottom line. Last year, the company avoided $1bn in costs with its phone trade-in program. Nine out of 10 used products brought into its stores get reused or remanu-factured. . . . The company has set a goal of collecting 90 percent of the devices it sells by 2017.[22]

Examples such as these exist in many industries. Unfortunately, there are many more examples of waste and inefficiency. We still use and dis-pose of far more resources than we conserve or recycle. A direct driver of this waste is the materialism that motivates our desire to consume.

Materialism

A characteristic of the developed world is that, as a general rule, our pos-sessions vastly exceed our needs on a day-to-day basis. Perhaps it is part of our genetic inheritance from our hunter-gatherer days, but, for some reason, we seem incapable of living within our means. It is not clear that we are more prosperous as a result. It is a pity that, given our obvious capability for ingenuity, we have created an economic system that impov-erishes as much as it enables:

> A quote from the former Vogue editor Diana Vreeland comes to mind: "Give 'em what they never knew they wanted." Fast-fashion retailers like H&M, Topshop and Forever 21 are great at hawking what we never knew we wanted. Not only that, they offer it at steadily reduced prices. . . . Quality is no longer an issue, because you need clothes to last just "until the next trend comes along."[23]

It is equally distressing that we are willing to place our superficial con-cern for material things above the wellbeing of other humans. In addition to wasted resources, there are social and human costs to the mass-production of cheap t-shirts. We may believe that it improves our lives to have some-one else do our hard work for us ("Today, the United States makes only

2 percent of the clothing its consumers purchase, compared with roughly 50 percent in 1990"),[24] but there is nothing sustainable (in a holistic sense) in manufacturing clothes thousands of miles away, shipping them to the West, all for under $10. Ultimately, we are all worse off as a result:

> The wastefulness encouraged by buying cheap and chasing the trends is obvious, but the hidden costs are even more galling. . . "disposable clothing" is damaging the environment, the economy and even our souls. . . . Have we somehow become disconnected from ourselves? If we don't stop to consider this, we may end up perpetually rushing out to buy more "stuff," never realizing what we truly need, genuinely want and cannot afford to waste.[25]

In terms of customer responses to firm behavior (a willingness to reward socially responsible behavior by favoring those firms that best meet societal expectations), we are constrained by our desire to consume, our insistence on convenience, and our fixation on price. In short, while there are any number of studies that suggest consumers are willing to buy green or socially responsible products, there are many others that suggest consumers are quite capable of saying one thing, while doing another.[26] Most individuals, when asked, want to believe they are ethical and also convince the person asking them that this is the case. When it comes time to purchase, however, we seem either to be unwilling or unable to put our ethical aspirations into practice. It seems that our best intentions are easily distracted and there is a limit for firms that rely too heavily on the market segment of ethical consumers:

> In the beginning, American Apparel put a "sweatshop free" label on its t-shirts. But sex turned out to be a better sell than good labor practices. Lessons in the limits of altruism.[27]

In spite of the success of brands like Seventh Generation, "green products of any brand account for less than 2 percent of the overall market."[28] In other words, the evidence suggests that ethical products remain a niche market:

> Everyone wants to buy "green" products, right? After all, we tell ourselves, we care about the environment and the resources left to

future generations. However, research shows that while 40 percent of consumers say they are willing to buy "green products," only 4 percent actually do so when given the option.[29]

Driving our materialism to new depths is the concept of *conspicuous virtue*—the idea that it is the perception of a good, rather than its functional value, that drives the consumption of that good. An example of this might be a consumer who drives a Prius primarily because they want to convey to others their concern for the environment. This focus on perceptions can rise to the point where it overrides the actual benefit to the environment that driving a Prius offers.[30] This idea also has parallels with what economists call a *Veblen good*—"a product that is valued and desirable simply for being more expensive." The idea of a Veblen good was introduced by Thorstein Veblen in 1899 in a sociological paper titled "Theory of the Leisure Class," which introduced the idea of conspicuous consumption. This idea can be twisted to highlight the idea of *conspicuous virtue*:

> Conspicuous consumption stays with us today. But increasingly, it seems [that] many consumers are not seeking an outright demonstration of wealth. Instead, they consume to demonstrate their innate goodness. They spend not to suggest the deepness of their pockets but the deepness of their hearts. We inhabit, to update Veblen, an age of conspicuous virtue.[31]

Conspicuous virtue arises when consumers purchase virtuous goods, in part, to demonstrate their virtuousness, rather than for the instrumental value of the goods themselves. The goal is "to make a statement. It is not only to do right, whatever that might mean, but to announce that you are doing so."[32] Cynics suggest that this idea of conspicuous virtue helps explain the consumption of goods such as the *Livestrong* yellow armband[33] that simultaneously raised money for cancer research, while allowing the donor (who had donated a very small amount) to demonstrate to the world that he or she supports the cause:

> More than 60 million have sold since 2004, one of the greatest successes in nonprofit fund-raising history, with the proceeds

going to cancer-related causes. No doubt some wear the bands in solidarity, or for inspiration—but, that said, the wristband conceit was simply ingenious. It allowed people to make a show of their virtue. They could give to a good cause, and they could advertise their caring to everyone else.[34]

Related to this issue of conspicuousness is the idea that the level of visibility of something (rather than its level of danger or seriousness, for example) largely determines our reaction to it. This phenomenon, discussed in terms of consumption previously, has an important application to the debate around sustainability and was most forcibly brought home during the Deepwater Horizon oil spill.[35] While the Deepwater spill deservedly caused a very strong negative reaction, there is a much more serious and long-lasting form of pollution in the Gulf of Mexico that continues, but is routinely ignored. It is caused by the phosphate and nitrogen run-off from fertilizers used in farms along the Mississippi river. The excess runs off into the river and then flows down to the Gulf, causing a dead zone that is much bigger and more damaging than the Deepwater Horizon oil spill. Because we cannot see it (and because of the strength of the farm lobby in Washington DC), however, it does not garner much media attention and even less public concern.[36] Similarly, while we get angry about rivers catching fire,[37] we cannot see the build-up of carbon dioxide (and many other pollutants) in the atmosphere, which helps explain why more people are not outraged about the problem and motivated to act.

Scale

In order to quantify the scale of the challenge humanity faces in creating a more sustainable economic system, it is instructive to understand not only the extent of the damage done to date, but, perhaps more importantly, the pace at which we continue to do harm:

> Everyone knows what must be done about climate change, but no one is doing anything about it. More than two decades of speeches and summitry have failed to thin out emissions of greenhouse gases. In fact, emissions are accelerating: a quarter of all the carbon

dioxide pumped into the air by humans was put there in the decade between 2000 and 2010. It will hang around for centuries, meaning that the future is sure to be hotter, even if all greenhouse-gas emissions cease overnight. The official ambition of limiting the global temperature rise to 2ºC looks increasingly like a bad joke.[38]

As a result of the enormity of the challenge, a large-scale response is required. *Large scale*, however, is not currently where we are at as a society:

Like recycling, re-using carrier bags has become something of an iconic "sustainable behaviour." But whatever else its benefits may be, it is not, in itself, an especially good way of cutting carbon. Like all simple and painless behavioural changes, its value hangs on whether it acts as a catalyst for other, more impactful, activities or support for political changes.[39]

Although changes such as recycling aluminum cans, or using reusable shopping bags, or buying fair-trade coffee, or changing light bulbs at home make us feel like we are taking action; in reality, we are not even scratching the surface of the problem. For the overall effect to be meaningful, the positive environmental actions need to outweigh the negative, need to do so worldwide, and need to touch all aspects of our lives. Unfortunately, we are far from achieving this. The danger, of course, is that, if we convince ourselves we are doing something, it reduces our willingness to make the difficult decisions that are necessary to generate meaningful reform. The solution, as with all the ideas discussed in this book, depends on stakeholders demanding change from companies and being willing to enforce that change:

Clearly, economic systems do not overhaul themselves—and in a democracy, majority support is a prerequisite for any significant societal shift. Politicians do not take risks if they don't think the electorate will support them. And civil society cannot function without a diverse supporter-base.[40]

The issues discussed in this principle (and indirectly throughout the book) rely on the assumption that society today owes an obligation to future generations to leave them a planet that is functional. If we accept this broad, intergenerational obligation, the question then becomes: *How much should we be willing to pay today to minimize the future costs of our current actions?* Long ago, Howard Bowen was thinking about "the responsibilities of a business toward future generations as distinct from the present generation" and the difficult tradeoffs involved:

> How rapidly and in what manner should it utilize nonreplaceable natural resources? What provision should be made for replacement of timber, fish, and other reproducible natural resources? Is the destruction of arable land through strip mining ethically defensible? These are extremely difficult questions because there are no clear principles to determine precisely how the interests of future generations should be balanced against those of present generations, or to what extent private business should be called upon to look out for future generations.[41]

This issue is particularly relevant in terms of issues such as climate change, but relates also to the broader issue of how to value future benefit against present-day cost. One recent attempt to do that was the Stern report on climate change,[42] which argued that society must "value the welfare of all present and future citizens equally and give no special preference to current voters."[43] The difficulty is, of course, how to account for the possibility of unknowns such as technical innovation and the greater wealth of future generations and, as a result, avoid exaggerating the immediate cost implications of climate change (and causing unnecessary present-day suffering). Tackling this balance between current and future obligations is crucial if we are to ensure an effective and realizable response to this hugely important issue:

> The problem of weighting the present and the future equally is that there is a lot of future. The number of future generations is potentially so large that small but permanent benefit to them would justify great sacrifice now. If we were to use this criterion to appraise all long-term investment, the volume of such investment would impoverish the current population. . . . The burden

of caring for all humanity, present and future, is greater than even the best-intentioned of us can bear.[44]

While it appears that our capacity for altruism toward future generations is limited, perhaps we can act to save ourselves. The speed at which climate change is occurring suggests that we will see dramatic changes to the environment in our lifetime. If so, sustainability increasingly represents a present-day imperative. Although this is potentially beneficial (in that it will motivate us to act, finally), meaningful change will most likely only come about in the face of impending doom. As such, it will require more dramatic change in a shorter timeframe and, already, the consequences are beginning to show. There is evidence that short bursts of severe weather can do significant damage to economic output,[45] for example, and that climate change is increasingly understood by business as "an economically disruptive force . . . that contributes to lower GDPs, higher food and commodity costs, broken supply chains and increased financial risk."[46]

With the huge implications for changes in behavior that will be required by people in both developed and developing countries, it is essential that buy-in is secured as quickly as possible and that corporations are recruited to help us mobilize. To this end, as Marc Gunther provocatively asks:

> Here's a question. Which trio of companies has done more for the environment . . . Patagonia, Starbucks and Chipotle? Or Walmart, Coca-Cola and McDonald's? . . . Patagonia, Starbucks and Chipotle have been path-breaking companies when it comes to sustainability, but Walmart, Coca-Cola and McDonald's are so much bigger that, despite their glaring flaws, and the fundamental problems with their business models, they will have a greater impact as they get serious about curbing their environmental footprint, and that of their suppliers.[47]

While provocative, the answer to the question is intuitive. That is not to say that the question isn't an important one to ask. Perhaps, for the CSR and sustainability community, it is the only question worth asking.

Ultimately, the core of the issue is: Are we interested in *ideal possibilities* or *meaningful change*? If *change* is what we want, then Walmart, Coca-Cola, and McDonald's need to be the source. That is not to diminish the wonderful business models of Patagonia, Starbucks, and Chipotle. If anything, they are the roadmap for what larger firms also need to accomplish. But, unless the largest companies are fully invested in *strategic CSR*, we will only be working at the periphery of the progress that needs to be made.

It is similar to the conundrum I face every time I recycle a plastic bottle—it is still the environmentally responsible thing to do, even though I am fully aware that the effect on the planet's future is limited, especially in light of the huge amount of resources that are wasted elsewhere in our economic system every day. It is not even clear that recycling results in less environmental impact. Just as building more roads encourages more people to drive and "recycling programs do increase recycling rates, studies have shown that they also increase total consumption."[48]

For-profit firms are the most important organizational form because it is only these organizations that can combine scarce resources in the most efficient way on the scale necessary to implement meaningful economic reform in the timeframe within which change needs to occur. Within the vast group of organizations labeled *for-profit firms*, however, there are some that contain vastly more potential for significant impact. Massive firms have a disproportionate impact on our daily lives. The market capitalization of the Top 10 global firms alone is $1.5 trillion.[49] What these large firms do in the near future, therefore, will do more to influence our lifestyles, standard of living, and future security than all of the smaller firms combined. As Jason Clay states in his TED talk on how big brands can save biodiversity:

> 100 companies control 25 percent of the trade of all 15 of the most significant commodities on the planet. . . . Why is 25 percent important? Because if these companies demand sustainable products they will pull 40–50 percent of production.[50]

According to Clay, it is all about the B2B supply chain. Suppliers are as important a stakeholder to the firm as the customer. Large companies pushing other large companies will achieve change much faster and on a scale that actually matters than waiting for consumers, one-by-one, to wake up to the global consequences of their consumption decisions.

Summary

Principle 8 states that *Scale matters; only business can save the planet.* The core argument rests on the idea that scale is essential—that the problem has reached a point where only substantial change will produce meaningful effects and help avert the catastrophic outcome we are otherwise hurtling toward. In this light, while for-profit firms are the main cause of the environmental mess we face; they are also the main hope for a solution. There is much work to do—both in terms of production and consumption—in order to create a truly *sustainable* economic system.

PRINCIPLE 9

Strategic CSR Is Not an Option; It *Is* Business

In brief: *Strategic CSR* is a philosophy of management that infuses the firm. All business decisions have economic, social, moral, and ethical dimensions. As such, all firms do *strategic CSR*, whether they realize it or not; it is just that some firms do it better than others.

As demonstrated by Principle 8, fundamental change on a massive scale (and quickly) is necessary if we are to make our economic system more sustainable. *Strategic CSR* provides an actionable solution to this problem, but only if the scope and scale of this managing philosophy are properly understood. *Strategic CSR* is not a peripheral activity; it is central to everything the firm does.

Not Philanthropy, but Core Operations

Strategic CSR is not about philanthropy;[1] it is about day-to-day operations. If any money is being spent by the firm on areas that are not directly related to core competencies, it is likely not the most efficient use of that money. If, however, the main justification for an expenditure is brand awareness and the firm feels there is value in being associated with a particular charity or good cause (in other words, if the values underpinning the cause align with those of the firm's stakeholders), then that investment should be made, but responsibility for it should be placed where it belongs, in the marketing department. The marketing department contains experts who know best how to manage the brand. If, however, there are other business-related reasons for the firm to donate money to a specific cause, then responsibility for that decision should lie with the relevant functional area—it should be part of the firm's core functions so that the relevant expertise can be applied for optimal, value-added effect.

The connection between CSR and philanthropy is tangential, at best. Although there are specific tax advantages associated with donations, the main reason for making the payment is the potential marketing-related benefits, if employed strategically. Unless there is a direct connection to business operations, the argument for firms donating large sums in areas in which they have low levels of expertise is difficult to make. One reason for this is that, not only is corporate philanthropy likely to be an inefficient use of resources if it is unrelated to core operations, but it can also go largely unrewarded (or even unrecognized) by the stakeholders it is designed to placate:

> Walmart is extremely generous, giving away over $1bn in cash and product annually—but it's still viewed by the public as one of the least responsible companies on the planet, and is a continual target of boycotts and protests. Wells Fargo donated over $315m in 2012, the most cash of any company in the nation, and even did so in a thoughtful manner, focusing on low-income housing and first-time homebuyer support—yet it still ranked as one of the 10 most disliked companies in America in 2013.[2]

Alternatively, consider what would happen if corporate America was willing to take the more than $18 billion it donates annually[3] and, instead, invest it in what it does best—operating its business?

> Imagine that [Walmart] didn't give away a billion dollars this year— and instead took that money, combined it with a negligible price increase, and paid all of its workers a living wage of $12 per hour. . . . The effort would improve the lives of its employees and families, save the economy hundreds of millions of dollars annually, and potentially change the way the public perceives Walmart.[4]

For-profit firms should focus on identifying problems for which there is a clear market-based solution and then deliver that solution in an efficient and socially responsible manner. The idea of *strategic CSR* as a managing philosophy focuses on firms' areas of expertise throughout all aspects of operations and de-emphasizes actions that stray outside a firm's areas of expertise, for which there either is not a market solution or the firm is not well-suited to deliver that solution. That is how value is optimized over the medium to long term—by operating in a way that seeks to meet the needs and demands of the firm's stakeholders, broadly defined. In other words, the focus of business remains the same; it is the way the organization goes about it that is different with a *strategic CSR* perspective.

Not Caring Capitalism, but Market Capitalism

In recent years, and particularly since the 2007–2008 financial crisis, there have been various attempts to reinvent capitalism. High profile actors, such as Bill Gates of Microsoft ("creative capitalism") and Muhammad Yunus of Grameen Bank ("social business") have sought to reform the underlying principles of capitalist ideology by urging firms to adopt goals beyond a focus on profit. More recently, work has begun to develop the concept of "inclusive capitalism, which is the idea that those with the power and the means have a responsibility to help make society stronger and more inclusive for those who don't."[5]

As discussed throughout this book, *strategic CSR* rejects these attempts as not only futile, but quite possibly counter-productive. It is not the ends of capitalism that matters so much as the means by which those ends are pursued.[6] Although efforts to alter the ends of capitalism are delivered with the best of intentions, the difficulties in implementation quickly become apparent when these ideas are investigated in a little more detail. Bill Gates, for example, launched his manifesto for a new system of capitalism in a speech at the World Economic Forum at Davos in 2008:

> I like to call this new system creative capitalism—an approach where governments, businesses, and nonprofits work together to stretch the reach of market forces so that more people can make a profit, or gain recognition, doing work that eases the world's inequities.[7]

While appealing at first glance, it is not clear what Gates actually means by creative capitalism and how it is to be realized in practice. For example, it is easy to say that:

> I hope corporations will consider dedicating a percentage of your top innovators' time to issues that could help people left out of the global economy. . . . It is a great form of creative capitalism, because it takes the brainpower that makes life better for the richest, and dedicates it to improving the lives of everyone else.[8]

But, in reality, how is a firm to decide which issue it should prioritize and devote its most valuable resources? How much value is compromised because these top innovators are working on a philanthropic problem (that may or may not be suited to their particular set of skills) instead of one based on market demand? How should firms determine exactly which projects are "appropriate" and which are not? Do firms need to calculate a certain level of potential "social goodness" in advance? How would they do that? What if it is not realized? None of these questions are addressed sufficiently, with Gates weaving back and forth between an argument based on market forces and one based on an appeal to the altruistic side of firms and their stakeholders without any clear guidance as to how priorities among competing claims should be set. As one supportive commentator noted:

> In Gates' vision, private companies should be encouraged to tweak their structure slightly to free up their innovative thinkers to work on solutions to problems in the developing world. It's gung-ho, rather than hairshirt, philanthropy. . . . While companies or individuals may ultimately profit from this work in developing nations, the reward primarily comes in the form of recognition and enjoyment.[9]

On an individual or microlevel, such arguments are appealing, romantic even; but, at a macrolevel, they quickly fall apart. I suggest the market, while imperfect, remains the best means society has for allocating scarce resources. As noted by a critic of caring capitalism:

> There is a stronger argument to be made against "creative capitalism," and it is that profits come from serving society. The larger the profits, the better job the company tends to have done. Profit maximization is a worthy goal by itself.[10]

Put more bluntly, *strategic CSR*, implemented throughout the firm via a stakeholder perspective and a focus on medium- to long-term value creation, optimizes performance:

> Sure, let those who have become rich under capitalism try to do good things for those who are still poor, as Mr. Gates has admirably chosen to do. But a New-Age blend of market incentives and feel-good recognition will not end poverty. History has shown that profit-motivated capitalism is still the best hope for the poor.[11]

Similar criticisms can be leveled against Muhammad Yunus, the 2006 winner of the Nobel Peace Prize, whose concept of social business touches on ideas similar to those expressed by Gates.[12] In reality, what both men are expressing is a form of social entrepreneurship, which demands that firms replace profit-seeking with something that amounts to altruism:

> "Social business" marks a transition from the imaginative to the quixotic, envisaging a new sector of the economy made up of companies run as private businesses but making no profits. These would focus on products and services that conventional companies do not find profitable, such as healthcare, nutrition, housing and sanitation for the poor. It is predicated on the view that investors will be happy to get zero return as long as they can see returns in social benefits.[13]

Such business models have limited market appeal—while some consumers are willing to pay the associated price premiums, the evidence suggests strongly that these same values cannot be assumed market-wide. In advocating such a philosophy, Yunus is turning his back on the sound business model for which he won his Nobel Prize. Microfinance (and Grameen Bank, the organization founded by Yunus to deliver microloans to individuals who could not secure them from mainstream financial institutions) is effective because it extends the market to consumers whose demand was thought to be insufficient for traditional finance models. All it took was a product tailored to the specific needs of a specific segment of the market. While microfinance is an industry that is grounded in business fundamentals (at least, as initially conceptualized), it is not clear how Yunus expects altruism to constitute sufficient incentive to mobilize the private sector as a whole:

> The genius of microfinance was in getting the profit motive to work for the very poorest. The drawback of social business is that it depends on the kindness of strangers.[14]

Not Sharing Value, but Creating Value

The ideas of creative capitalism and social business present leaps of faith and logic that are similar to those generated by the idea of shared value. Similar to Gates and Yunus, Michael Porter and Mark Kramer have enjoyed a significant amount of publicity for their idea, which also attempts to overturn centuries of economic theory and practice to reinvent the firm:

> The purpose of the corporation must be redefined as creating shared value, not just profit per se.[15]

On the surface, Porter's shared value (or caring capitalism) and *strategic CSR* can appear to produce similar behavior. The motivating force is different, however, and this is important because it will lead to different outcomes in terms of the venture's ultimate success or failure. The difference comes down to the focus of the firm and the relevance to core operations of the issue at hand. Starbucks, for example, should not form partnerships with shade-grown coffee farmers in Guatemala because it recognizes those farmers face an uncertain future with an insufficient welfare net to support them if their businesses fail (a nonoperational goal), but because Starbucks needs to secure a stable supply of high quality coffee beans and supporting these farmers in a sustainable manner is the best way to guarantee that supply (an operational goal). In other words, Starbucks should form stable and lasting partnerships with these key suppliers not because it is seeking to fill a charitable need, the firm should do it because these farmers produce a raw material that is essential to its business. Starbucks is incentivized to protect the raw material in a sustainable way, rather than ruthlessly exploit it. If those Guatemalan farmers are not producing a product that is in demand (i.e., if the business logic for a relationship is not there), the argument that Starbucks should get involved is difficult to make.

Ultimately, although for-profit firms can help with the first perspective (caring capitalism), they are much better suited to the second perspective (market capitalism). Ideally, it is the role of governmental and nonprofit sectors to focus on those areas that the market ignores or cannot solve. In contrast, Porter and Kramer argue that charitable goals should be considered equally with operational goals and firms should then utilize their market-based skills and expertise to solve both kinds of problem— in other words, that they should become less like for-profit firms and more like social entrepreneurs, government agencies, or nonprofit organizations. While well-intentioned, I believe that this is not an effective plan for "how to fix capitalism" and, instead, indicates a fundamental misunderstanding of the value of for-profit firms in our society (and of the role that a *strategic CSR* perspective brings in optimizing that value). As suggested by other critics of these attempts to reinvent capitalism:[16]

> In her 2009 book SuperCorp, . . . Rosabeth Moss Kanter warned of the pitfalls for companies that make "social commitments that do not have an economic logic that sustains the enterprise by attracting resources." More companies are learning to reap commercial benefits from strategies that have a wider social value. That's great. But the basic job of coaxing capitalism in the right direction is the same as it always has been: find ways to harness society's needs to companies' self-interest and hope the two stay together.[17]

While there is certainly an important role for social entrepreneurs in CSR, it is naive to suggest that all companies should exist primarily to solve problems motivated by altruism. Business is the solution to market problems or opportunities that create value as a direct consequence. Firms optimize value, broadly defined, by combining scarce and valuable resources to meet market needs, while considering the interests of a broad range of stakeholders and seeking to provide sustainable shareholder returns over the medium to long term. Firms can often use their expertise to assist in meeting nonoperational goals, but this should not be their primary concern. Governments and nonprofits also play important social roles where gaps in the market occur.

The difference between a firm with *strategic CSR* integrated fully throughout the organization (encompassing strategic decision making and all aspects of day-to-day operations) and a firm that ignores the ideas discussed in this book is not whether its CEO donates to charity, but is reflected in the way the firm operates the core aspects of its business. There is a more socially responsible way to produce your products, to treat your suppliers, to pay your employees, and to comply with laws, for example, and there is a less responsible way of doing all these things. Those firms that seek to act responsibly through a *strategic CSR* perspective are adding more value than any amount of philanthropy can achieve.

CSR Is Not an Option

The consequence of internalizing the previous discussion is the realization that *CSR is not an option*. It is not an option because CSR, or at least *strategic CSR*, is not about philanthropy, and is more than brand insurance;[18] it is not about caring capitalism and is not about sharing value. *Strategic CSR* is about the firm's core operations—creating value for stakeholders, broadly defined, by focusing on the firm's areas of expertise to solve market-based problems.

Because the scale and scope of *strategic CSR* is so thoroughly embedded within core operations and everyday decisions, it is not something the firm can choose to do (or not do); it is the way business is conducted. When a firm hires an employee, engages with a supplier, responds to a regulator, sells a product, or does any one of the many things it does every day, it is engaging in *strategic CSR*. All of these business decisions have economic, social, moral, and ethical dimensions. As such, *strategic CSR* is not something that can be ignored or relegated in importance—it is what firms do; it is just that some firms do it better and more deliberately than others. Vigilant and informed stakeholders who enforce their values onto organizations will ensure that this measure of performance (the extent to which the firm performs better at *strategic CSR*) will increasingly become a predictor of market success.

Once firms understand that they are embedded in complex stakeholder relations and that they need to manage these relations effectively if they are to survive and thrive over the medium to long term in today's global business environment, then strategic planning and daily operations represent the means to manage the messy trade-offs and priority-setting. Certainly, firms are either better or worse at managing these relationships and they draw the lines of key stakeholders narrowly (at shareholders alone) or more broadly (in terms of a wider group of constituents). Either way, however, CSR is not an option, it is the way that business is conducted in the twenty-first century. Understanding and applying the underlying principles detailed in this book will help firms be more effective at implementing *strategic CSR* and building a sustainable organization for the medium to long term.

Summary

Principle 9 states that *Strategic CSR is not an option; it* is *business*. *Strategic CSR* is a management philosophy that is intricately woven into every decision the firm makes. It is not about peripheral activities, such as philanthropy, but about how the firm treats its employees and suppliers and customers, and all of its stakeholders. It is not about being compassionate or sharing value; it is about a firm doing what it does best—applying its area of technical expertise to build a competitive advantage that enables it to solve a market-based problem (from which society greatly benefits). As such, *strategic CSR* is not an option, it is integral to all aspects of operations. There is simply no choice to be made. All firms do *strategic CSR* (like all firms do strategy, marketing, and so on)—it is just that some do it better than others.

Milton Friedman Was Right; the Social Responsibility of Business Is *Business*

In brief: Milton Friedman believed that the firm should focus on economic success. *Strategic CSR* is not about peripheral issues, but day-to-day decisions and core operations. Above all, it argues that the pursuit of profit over the medium- to long term optimizes value creation. Business serves society best when it focuses primarily on *business*.

As indicated in Principle 9, *strategic CSR* is not about issues that are peripheral to the firm and is not about reinventing capitalism. Rather, it is about improving day-to-day decisions that focus on core operations and creating value, broadly defined. As a result, I believe that *strategic CSR*, as a management philosophy, is fully compatible with Milton Friedman's belief that business serves society best when it focuses primarily on *business*.

The Business of Business Is Business

Milton Friedman was right—the social responsibility of business is *business*. In Friedman's own words, what he meant by this is that:

> In a free-enterprise, private-property system, a corporate executive is an employee of the owners of the business. He has direct responsibility to his employers. That responsibility is to conduct the business in accordance with their desires, which generally will be to make as much money as possible *while conforming to the basic rules of the society, both those embodied in law and those embodied in ethical custom.* [emphasis added][1]

Friedman argued, essentially, that conducting business in a way that produces the best possible outcomes for the firm's shareholders in the long run involves playing by the rules of the game. And, although he did not say it directly, he recognizes that it is the firm's stakeholders, collectively, who determine those rules. *Strategic CSR* conforms to this economic view.

Stakeholders have always shaped the rules by which society operates, consciously or otherwise, and they will continue to do so. The questions that are essential for any manager to ask, therefore, are *What are the rules today?* and *What are they likely to be tomorrow?* The rules are always changing, but the aggregate effect of millions of people making millions of decisions everyday determines the overall parameters within which firms must act. Corporations cannot force consumers to buy their products, as long as consumers are willing to make their purchase decisions based on something other than convenience or the lowest price. Similarly, corporations cannot prevent the enactment of legislation, as long as politicians are willing to prioritize governing over campaign contributions and lobbying pressures. And corporations cannot force employees to work for abusive pay levels, as long as workers ensure they have the skill set to demand higher pay and better conditions. Each of these decisions is a value judgment made by one of the firm's stakeholders. Managers, therefore, need to understand the values that underpin these decisions at any given point in time because they have operational consequences for the firm. Those managers who understand the rules most completely are best placed to help their organization succeed by aligning the firm's actions with the underlying values of its stakeholders.

While the business of business is business, the goal of this book has been to build the argument that how this *business* is conducted matters. The concept of *strategic CSR*, therefore, constitutes a roadmap for the executive seeking to conduct business successfully in the twenty-first century because, rather than obsess about what the firm does (generate profits), *strategic CSR* is more focused on how the firm does it. In other words, framing the argument is key, and policies or practices that lower costs, raise revenues, or both over the medium to long term are of primary importance. In order to illustrate this, let's return to the debate between a living wage and a minimum wage: Does a firm pay its employees a living wage because it feels that they deserve something better, or does it pay them a living wage because it understands that the investment raises morale and loyalty, increases productivity, and decreases the recruitment and training costs that are associated with higher turnover? As Paul Polman, CEO of Unilever puts it:

> To pay a textile worker in Pakistan 11 cents an hour doesn't make good business sense. . . . [Before I became CEO] We had a lot of contingent labour or we outsourced it and we looked at that as a cost item but we had a tremendous amount of turnover. Now we pay more and we have greater loyalty, more energy and higher productivity.[2]

Similarly, as discussed in Principle 9: Does a firm like Starbucks pay its suppliers of high-quality, shade-grown Arabica beans an above-market price because it feels morally or ethically responsible for farmers that do not earn sufficient wages in a country with an inadequate welfare safety-net, or does it pay those fair trade prices because it needs to secure a guaranteed supply of its most essential raw material? Whether you think of Starbucks as a café or as a third place between home and work, the firm risks its core business if it loses access to high-quality coffee beans. As such, it is in Starbucks' best strategic interest to ensure the producers of its most highly prized raw material are incentivized to remain in business and continue to supply the firm over the long term.

These ideas and the underlying philosophy that drives them are wholly consistent with Friedman's work.

Milton Friedman

Although Milton Friedman wrote many books and articles in his career, perhaps the one for which he is best known (and most widely cited) within the CSR community is the article he published in *The New York Times Magazine* in 1970, "The Social Responsibility of Business is to Increase its Profits."[3] In the article, in which the economist is at his inflammatory best, Friedman argues that profit, as a result of the firm's actions, is an end in itself. He believes strongly that a firm need not have any additional justification for existing and that, in fact, social value is maximized when firms focus solely on pursuing their self-interest by attempting to generate profit:

> I share Adam Smith's skepticism about the benefits that can be expected from "those who affected to trade for the public good." . . . in a free society, . . . "there is one and only one social responsibility of business—to use its resources and engage in activities designed to increase its profits."[4]

Friedman's article is often contrasted against a 2002 article in *Harvard Business Review*, titled "What's a Business For?" by the influential British management commentator, Charles Handy.[5] In contrast to Friedman, Handy presents a much broader view of the role of business in society. For Handy, it is not sufficient to justify a firm's profits as an end in itself. For Handy, a business has to have a motivation other than merely making money to justify its existence—profit is merely a means to achieve a larger end, which is some form of social good. A firm should not remain in existence just because it is profitable, but because it is meeting a need that society *as a whole* values:

> It is salutary to ask about any organization, "If it did not exist, would we invent it? Only if it could do something better or more useful than anyone else" would have to be the answer, and profit would be the means to that larger end.[6]

On the surface, the positions taken by Friedman and Handy appear to be irreconcilable and that is how they are often treated by the CSR community. Indeed, Friedman seems to go out of his way to antagonize CSR advocates by arguing that socially responsible behavior is a waste of the firm's resources, which legally (in his view, cf. Principle 2) belong to the firm's shareholders and not the firm's managers:

> That is why, in my book *Capitalism and Freedom*, I have called [social responsibility] a "fundamentally subversive doctrine" in a free society.[7]

But, on closer analysis, my interpretation is that their arguments are not nearly as far apart as they initially appear. Incorporating the ideas underpinning *strategic CSR* narrows the gap between these two authors considerably. First, it is necessary to ask: If the purpose of the firm is to meet a need that society, as a whole, values (as Handy argues), what is the best means we have of quantifying that value? As discussed in Principle 6, *profit* is by far the most accurate means we have of estimating that value—not perfect, but it is difficult to imagine a more complete measure. If true, then surely the most profitable firms are adding the most value (as Friedman argues). Again, the correlation is not perfect, but, as a general rule, the relationship between profit and value should hold.

Second, for additional consideration that Friedman and Handy are not as far apart as many believe, consider the following two questions:

- Does it make sense for a large financial firm to donate money to a group researching the effects of climate change because the CEO believes this is an important issue?
- Does it make sense for an oil firm to donate money to the same group because it perceives climate change as a threat to its business model and wants to mitigate that threat by investigating possible alternatives?

The action, a large for-profit firm donating money to a nonprofit group, is the same. The difference is the relevance of the nonprofit's activities to the firm's core operations. Most level-headed CSR advocates would at least question the first action as a potential waste of money (incorporating Friedman's argument that the actions represent an inefficient allocation of resources in an area in which the firm has no expertise), while the second action is a strategic question for a firm that needs to address issues that are important to key stakeholder groups in its operating environment.

Taking the arguments of Friedman and Handy in their entirety, therefore, a more insightful interpretation suggests that, to the extent that it is in a firm's interests to meet the needs of its key stakeholders (who determine their own positions and actions based on a complicated mix of ethics, values, and self-interest), the firm should do so. And, perhaps more importantly, that, by doing so, the firm can deliver the greatest value to the widest range of its stakeholders. From Handy's perspective, this point is easy to argue, but Friedman also recognizes this. He qualifies his statement that a manager's primary responsibility is to the shareholders of the enterprise, who seek "to make as much money as possible," for example, by noting that this pursuit must be tempered "while conforming to the basic rules of the society, *both those embodied in law and those embodied in ethical custom.*" In addition, a firm's actions are acceptable, only as long as it "engages in open and free competition *without deception or fraud*"[8] (emphasis added).

In qualifying his statements in this way (leaving a loophole in his argument big enough to drive any ethical or moral bus through), Friedman clearly outlines a responsibility for business to conform to society's expectations. And, in contrast to the inflammatory rhetoric he often used to convey his points, he is allowing for those societal expectations that are expressed both formally, in law, and informally, in norms and everyday conventions. Given that the ends of the organization that Handy portrays are to reinforce the values of the societies in which it operates, the similarities between the two men become even more apparent.

This overlap was also noted by Archie Carroll, one of the most important thinkers on CSR, in his pivotal 1991 *Business Horizons* article that details his idea of the four corporate responsibilities in the "Pyramid of CSR":

> Economist Milton Friedman . . . has argued that social matters are not the concern of business people and that these problems should be resolved by the unfettered workings of the free market system. Friedman's argument loses some of its punch, however, when you consider his assertion in its totality. . . . Most people focus on the first part of Friedman's quote but not the second part. It seems clear from this statement that profits, conformity to the law, and ethical custom embrace three components of the CSR pyramid—economic, legal, and ethical. That only leaves the philanthropic component for Friedman to reject. Although it may be appropriate for an economist to take this view, one would not encounter many business executives today who exclude philanthropic programs from their firms' range of activities.[9]

Rather than the result of this softening being presented as a reason for Friedman's argument to lose "some of its punch," however, I would argue that it reinforces the importance of incorporating Friedman's ideas within the intellectual framework underpinning *strategic CSR*.

The Business of Business Is *Strategic* CSR

As long as an argument can be made that any particular decision is in the best business interests of the firm, then I believe that is something that Milton Freidman would agree lies within the definition of *business*. In other words, while this book does not represent any kind of endorsement of Friedman's complete economic perspective (which is extremely comprehensive and would require a much more detailed investigation), it does argue that *strategic CSR* is compatible with the economic argument that all of a company's actions should reinforce its economic interests. As such, *strategic CSR*, built on a foundation of iterative, long-term relations with the firm's broad range of stakeholders, offers managers a roadmap to survive and thrive in today's complex, dynamic business environment.

To be sure, the philosophy of *strategic CSR* is demanding. It requires stakeholders to act in order to shape society in their collective interests. It also requires firms to respond to these demands and, where possible, to anticipate them. But, again, as long as stakeholders are willing to enforce their values and beliefs, conforming to those expectations is in the firm's economic self-interest. It is a responsibility that all of the firm's stakeholders (i.e., all of us) should take seriously. After all, the stakes are high and we are all invested in the future.

Strategic CSR is not a passive philosophy; it is proactive, but the result is a society that is *shaped*, rather than one that *forms*. If stakeholders are motivated to change the rules in a way that promotes value, broadly defined, then for-profit firms are the best means we have of interpreting those new standards and responding more rapidly and efficiently than any other organizational form in any other economic system.

Summary

Principle 10 states that *Milton friedman was right; the social responsibility of business is* business. It argues that *strategic CSR* is not about issues peripheral to the firm, but instead focuses on day-to-day decisions, strategic planning, and core operations. Equally important, it does so in a way that accounts for the complex, dynamic business environment in which firms today must operate. As such, *strategic CSR* is a philosophy of management that is designed to generate business success. And, because this success (i.e., profit) optimizes value when the firm meets the needs and demands of its broad range of stakeholders, it is compatible with Milton Friedman's arguments that firms benefit society the most when they focus on the business of business.

CONCLUSION

Strategic CSR As Value Creation

The ideas detailed in this book revolve around a set of defining principles that are designed to build an intellectual framework in support of *strategic CSR*. That is, in a dynamic environment that is defined by the actions and decisions of a firm's broad set of stakeholders, value is optimized when the stakeholders are willing to convey and enforce their needs to the firm, while the firm is willing to respond and, where possible, anticipate those changing needs. As such, these economic and social exchanges, at their most fundamental, are interactions formed around the collective set of values that are prevalent in society at any given point in time and are best measured by the profit the firm is able to generate.

The 10 Defining Principles of *Strategic* CSR

Principle 1   **Business equals social progress:** There is a direct correlation between the amount of business in a society and the extent of progress enjoyed by that society. For-profit firms are the most effective means of achieving that progress.

Principle 2   **Shareholders do not own the firm:** Contrary to popular myth, shareholders do not own the firm. Similarly, managers and directors do not have a fiduciary responsibility to maximize shareholder value. Instead, the firm should be run in the interests of its broad range of stakeholders.

Principle 3   **Identifying stakeholders is easy; prioritizing stakeholder interests is difficult:** Implementing *strategic CSR* requires the firm to operate in the interests of a broad range of stakeholders. While identifying a firm's stakeholders is easy, however, stakeholder theory will only be of practical value when it helps managers prioritize among competing stakeholder interests.

Principle 4   **CSR is not solely a *corporate* responsibility:** CSR will only work if firms are rewarded for acting and punished for failing to act. As such, while CSR includes a *responsibility* for a firm to meet the needs and demands of its stakeholders, the stakeholders themselves have an equal, if not more important, *responsibility* to hold the firm to account.

Principle 5   **Market-based solutions are optimal:** In general, market forces generate superior outcomes than alternative means of allocating scarce and valuable resources, such as government mandate. While stakeholders have an interest in shaping the behavior of for-profit firms, the mechanism by which this occurs most effectively is the market.

Principle 6   **Profit = economic value + social value:** A firm's profit represents the ability to sell a good or service at a higher price than what it costs to produce. Production and consumption, however, are more than merely technical decisions. They encapsulate the total value (economic and social) that is added by the firm.

Principle 7   **The *free* market is an illusion:** The free market is not *free*. It encourages firms to externalize costs that are then borne by society rather than consumers; it is rife with subsidies and quotas that favor some firms and industries over others. The result is an economic system that is distorted and, as a result, unsustainable.

Principle 8   **Scale matters; only business can save the planet:** The environmental challenge has reached the point where consumer driven change is insufficient. While for-profit firms were the main cause of the problem, they are also the main hope for a solution. Scale is vital and large firms must do much more if we are to create a sustainable economic system.

Principle 9   ***Strategic CSR* is not an option; it *is* business:** *Strategic CSR* is a philosophy of management that infuses the firm. All business decisions have economic, social, moral, and ethical dimensions. As such, all firms do *strategic CSR*, whether they realize it or not; it is just that some firms do it better than others.

Principle 10   **Milton Friedman was right; the social responsibility of business is *business*:** Milton Friedman believed that the firm should focus on economic success. *Strategic CSR* is not about peripheral issues, but day-to-day decisions and core operations. Above all, it argues that the pursuit of profit over the medium- to long term optimizes value creation. Business serves society best when it focuses primarily on *business*.

In conclusion, therefore, given the discussion of ideas and concepts in this book, how can we combine these 10 core principles into a succinct definition of *strategic CSR*?

Strategic CSR

The goal of this book has been to frame *strategic CSR* in terms of a set of principles that differentiate it from related concepts, such as sustainability and business ethics. While *sustainability* relates to issues of ecological preservation and *business ethics* seeks to construct normative prescriptions of *right* and *wrong*, *strategic CSR* is a pragmatic philosophy that is grounded, first and foremost, in the day-to-day operations of the firm. As such, *strategic CSR* is central to the firm's value creating activities and, ultimately, its success in today's global, dynamic business environment.

In constructing a working definition of *strategic CSR* that draws upon the ten underlying principles, five components are essential: First, that firms incorporate a CSR perspective within their culture and strategic planning process; second, that any actions they take are directly related to core operations; third, that they seek to understand and respond to the needs of their stakeholders; fourth, that they aim to optimize value delivered; and fifth, that they shift from a short-term perspective to managing their resources and relations with key stakeholders over the medium to long term.

Strategic CSR[1]

The incorporation of a holistic *CSR perspective* within a firm's strategic planning and *core operations* so that the firm is managed in the interests of a broad set of *stakeholders* to *optimize value* over the *medium to long term*.

Essential to any definition of *strategic CSR* is that firms incorporate a CSR perspective within their organizational culture and strategic planning process. This CSR perspective presupposes an iterative relationship between the firm and its stakeholders, with equal responsibilities to both convey needs and respond to those needs whenever possible (see Principle 4). An important tool that helps the firm do this is a *CSR filter* that is integrated throughout the firm's culture and operational decision-making processes. The CSR filter is defined as a conceptual screen through which strategic and tactical decisions are evaluated for their impact on the firm's various stakeholders.[2] Embedding the profit incentive within a framework of guiding values that set the parameters of decisions and guide all employees through the construction of the firm's strategy, helps managers implement *strategic CSR* throughout all aspects of day-to-day operations.[3]

The second component of *strategic CSR* is that any action a firm takes should be directly related to core operations (see Principle 10). In short, the same action will differ from firm-to-firm in terms of whether it can be classified as *strategic CSR*, depending on the firm's expertise and the relevance of the issue to the organization's vision and mission. *Strategic CSR* is not about activities that are peripheral to the firm, such as philanthropy; it is also not about redefining or reinventing capitalism; it is about the operational decisions that the firm makes day-in and day-out (see Principle 9). All aspects of business decisions involve economic, social, moral, and ethical considerations and the primary role of the manager is to balance these considerations in prioritizing the diverse set of interests that have a stake in the firm's operations from decision-to-decision (see principles 1 and 3). As such, the pursuit of business is, by definition, ethics and morals in action.

The third component of *strategic CSR* is that firms incorporate a stakeholder perspective throughout the firm. A barrier to the implementation of a stakeholder perspective, however, is the primary emphasis currently given by many corporations to the interests of its shareholders. Firms need to expand their view of stakeholders beyond shareholders (who neither own the firm, nor deserve any special attention from management and the board), to include all of the firm's stakeholders who, collectively, define the firm's operating environment (see Principle 2). In doing so, however, the firm has a responsibility not only to respond to stakeholder concerns, but also to anticipate these concerns whenever possible. For their part, stakeholders should be willing to enforce their needs onto firms by actively discriminating in favor of those firms that best match expectations. By managing the firm in the interests of its broad range of stakeholders, the firm increases its chances of creating a sustainable competitive advantage.

The fourth component of *strategic CSR* relates to the drive to *optimize* (as opposed to *maximize*) value, broadly defined (see Principle 6). In essence, the goal is to seek a balance between the production and consumption activities in society in order to build a standard of living that meets the needs of the collective. The production component includes incorporating costs that firms currently seek to externalize, while the consumption component includes incorporating costs that society currently seeks to avoid (see principles 5 and 7). If we can achieve this balance, and spread both the benefits and the costs over a wide range of stakeholders, we will be significantly closer to optimizing value throughout society.

The final, and perhaps most important, component of *strategic CSR* is the shift from a short-term perspective when managing the firm's resources and stakeholder relations to a medium- or long-term perspective. If managers alter their horizons from the next quarter or next season to the next decade or beyond, they immediately alter the priorities by which they manage and, as a result, automatically change the nature of the decisions they make today (see principles 2 and 8). If a CEO is only interested in the next quarter, it is difficult to make the case for *strategic CSR*. But, if the CEO is concerned with the continued existence of the firm 5, 10, or 20 years from now, the value of building lasting, trust-based relationships with key stakeholders increases exponentially.

These five components combine the ideas and concepts contained within the ten principles and define *strategic CSR*. In short: Principle 1 identifies the for-profit firm as the most important organizational form; Principle 2 locates stakeholder theory as central to operations; Principle 3 recognizes that it is the ability to prioritize stakeholder interests that is paramount for managers in practice; Principle 4 establishes the importance of corporate *stakeholder* responsibility; Principle 5 reminds us of the preeminent role of the market in constructing optimal solutions; Principle 6 notes that economic and social value are not independent of each other, but are highly correlated; Principle 7 argues that we have a long way to go before we can claim to have established a truly free market; Principle 8 highlights the importance of scale to achieving sustainable longevity; Principle 9 states that *strategic CSR* is not a choice, but integral to all aspects of strategic planning and day-to-day operations; and Principle 10 reinforces the central idea of Milton Friedman—that business optimizes value when it focuses on *business*, as detailed by the previous nine principles.

Combining these ten principles, the five components of *strategic CSR* are realized through a series of three conscious shifts that the firm's executive team must make:

1. **Shift from the periphery to the core.** As indicated earlier, CSR is not about philanthropy, it is about core operations. As such, a *strategic CSR* perspective or CSR filter needs to be applied to every major decision the firm takes. Culture is key, along with leadership from the top. As long as the CEO understands that CSR is central to the firm's ability to create value, then it immediately becomes central to his or her job.

2. **Shift from an externally oriented justification to an internally oriented justification.** The main value of CSR comes from its operational implications, not the reputational benefits. Whatever else one thinks about the sustainability of Walmart's business model, the firm's progressive work on resource utilization directly supports its business-level strategy of cost minimization. Whether Walmart's customers are aware of the logistical advances the firm is making seems less important to managers than the cost implications and knowledge that flow from the efficiencies they are creating in the supply chain. Their customers benefit from these innovations in terms of lower prices.

3. **Shift from short-term to long-term decision making.** It matters intensely whether the CEO and senior managers are building the firm for the long term versus aiming to meet analysts' quarterly projections. If someone is entering into a one-time exchange versus planning for the longer term, it automatically changes the overriding priorities and the decisions that are made today. For the firm, this

shift translates into a focus on building stronger relationships of trust with its wide range of stakeholders.

Sustainable Value Creation

Strategic CSR delivers an operational and strategic advantage to the firm. As such, it is central to the goal of value creation, which is the primary purpose of a firm's top management. *Strategic CSR* is a subtle tweak of our economic model that has radical implications. It will increasingly become the most effective way for firms to create value in the business environment of the 21st century.

In essence, *strategic CSR* represents an enlightened approach to management that retains the focus on adding value that is emphasized by a traditional bottom-line business model. Importantly, however, *strategic CSR* incorporates a commitment to meet the needs and demands of the firm's broad range of stakeholder groups. Equally important, in order to implement *strategic CSR* comprehensively, the focus of the firm has to be on optimizing value over the long term by acting in areas in which it has expertise (related to core operations).

This focus on long-term added value is the principal difference between a traditional shareholder-focused business model and a *strategic CSR* model integrated throughout operations. This shift in perspective (from short to long term) is relatively easy to envision, but much more difficult to implement firm-wide. Nevertheless, this shift alone brings a firm significantly closer to building a competitive advantage that is truly sustainable. *Strategic CSR*, therefore, is as simple (and as complex) as conducting all aspects of business operations in a responsible manner. It involves incorporating this perspective into the strategic planning processes of the firm in ways that optimize value.

Strategic CSR focuses on evolution, not revolution, working within what we know about human psychology and economic exchange. As such, *strategic CSR* encapsulates the way humans behave and business is conducted. It does not alter the goals of the firm (profit, except to say that a short-term focus is counter-productive) and it does not alter our understanding of fundamental economic theory (actors pursuing their self-interest can optimize value, broadly defined). What it does do, is alter the perspective from which operational and strategic decisions are made.

Do the managers of the firm believe they can optimize performance by paying the firm's employees a *minimum* wage (because there is sufficient unemployment that, if one employee leaves, they can hire another one), for example, or do the managers believe that they can optimize performance by paying the firm's employees a *living* wage (because it raises morale and productivity, while decreasing turnover rate and the hiring costs associated with replacing workers)? These two positions are substantively different approaches to business. Good arguments can be made in defense of both positions, but they are fundamentally different. This is the arena in which *strategic CSR* operates. It is a progressive, enlightened approach to management that places the interests of a wide-range of stakeholders within the decision matrix of the firm.[4]

The essential difference between those firms that do *strategic CSR* well and those that do it badly, therefore, is a greater sensitivity to the needs and concerns of the firm's broad range of stakeholders. This provides the firm with an acute ability to understand when the (stakeholder-defined) rules that define the firm's operational environment have changed, and a framework within which to apply that knowledge to the firm's strategic advantage. Those firms that can respond to (and, ideally, anticipate) those changes are better placed to survive and thrive in a dynamic business environment. Also, in striving to meet the needs and concerns of their stakeholders, those firms that engage in these activities in a more genuine, authentic way will find that the associated benefits are sustained because the effort is more effective and valued.

A short-term focus, driven by quarterly earnings guidance to investors with little long-term interest in the organization's survival, is of little concern (and is most likely detrimental) to firms committed to implementing *strategic CSR*. Similarly, while economic value and social value cover similar ground, the overlap is not perfect. Externalities and transgressions are the result. Values help fill the gap and aid the *strategic CSR* decision-making process.[5] To this end, the CSR filter is the tool the firm can use to apply its values to identify both potential opportunities and potential problems before they arise. The firm retains the societal legitimacy to remain an ongoing entity by seeking to implement its strategic plan and conduct operations while considering the needs and concerns of a broad array of stakeholders. The result is that, rather than profit maximization through a short-term focus, profit optimization emphasizes the importance of meeting the needs of these stakeholders over the medium to long term.

Strategic CSR, therefore, refines the economic system in which capitalism drives social and economic progress. The effects enhance the magnificent potential of business to alter our lives that has been summarized by the greatest minds of our time:

> *Profit for a company is like oxygen for a person. If you don't have enough of it, you're out of the game. But if you think your life is about breathing, you're really missing something.*
>
> —Peter Drucker[6]

> *Being the richest man in the cemetery doesn't matter to me. . . . Going to bed at night saying we've done something wonderful . . . that's what matters to me.*
>
> —Steve Jobs[7]

In short, *strategic CSR* equals value creation in today's complex and dynamic business environment—*sustainable* value creation. What does this mean in practice? Primarily, it means that those firms that "get" *strategic CSR* will be able to create more value over a longer period of time than those firms that either do not understand the strategic value of CSR to the firm or ignore it altogether.

Final Thoughts

As noted many years ago by Howard Bowen, the process of reorienting capitalism to better suit the interests of society, broadly defined, is a complex process "which goes to the very root of our basic social and economic philosophy."[8] As a result, this task will not be achieved overnight. Given that we are working to reform a system that is already well-equipped to generate phenomenal economic and social progress, however, the task is also not unimaginable:

> The development of a moral code for business that can win wide acceptance and social sanction necessarily involves somewhat the

same evolutionary process as characterizes the development of the law. . . . We should not assume, however, that we are starting in this process from zero. Even under laissez faire, there was a system of moral rules for business.[9]

Much of what makes capitalism such a successful system already accommodates the complex web of norms, customs, and practices that are shaped by the values we share as a progressive, democratic society. Since Bowen wrote these words in 1953, these core moral values have been the source of a vast literature detailing the social responsibilities of corporations and the managers who run them. The concept of *strategic CSR* is designed to contribute to this discussion and, hopefully, advance the debate toward the outcome that all those involved in the battle of ideas to improve our society wish to see.

About the Author

David Chandler (david.chandler@ucdenver.edu) is assistant professor of management and co-director of the managing for sustainability program at the University of Colorado Denver. His research focuses on the dynamic interface between the organization and its institutional environment. He is also interested in the relationship between institutions and values, and how organizational actions reflect values that sustain meaningful institutions. Empirically, he focuses on studying organizations within the context of corporate social responsibility, business ethics, and firm and stakeholder relations. Related publications include the textbook *Strategic Corporate Social Responsibility: Stakeholders, Globalization, and Sustainable Value Creation* (3rd edition, Sage Publications, Inc., 2014). He received his PhD in Management in 2011 from The University of Texas at Austin.

Notes

Epigraph

1. Brandeis (1912, November 23), p. 7.
2. Friedman (1962), chapter VIII, p. 133.

Introduction

1. In his well-known 1970 *New York Times Magazine* article in which he declared CSR to be a "fundamentally subversive doctrine," Milton Friedman built part of his argument around the idea that "Only people can have responsibilities. . . . 'business' as a whole cannot be said to have responsibilities." Putting aside the idea that a for-profit firm in our society can have *rights* (which Friedman recognizes and is not generally disputed) but not *responsibilities* (which Friedman dismisses and is disputed), in this book, the organization is the actor of primary focus. As such, I will refer to firms as entities that, for example, can 'act in their own best interest.' While I do not seek to anthropomorphize corporations, in order to discuss their social responsibility, it is necessary to separate the collective (the company) from the individuals who act on its behalf (executives, directors, and employees).
2. Bader (2014).
3. See: Alexander Dahlsrud, 'How Corporate Social Responsibility is Defined: An Analysis of 37 Definitions,' *Corporate Social Responsibility and Environmental Management*, Vol. 15, 2008, pp. 1–13.
4. Aguinis and Glavas (2012).
5. Devinney (2009).
6. See, Dahlsrud (2008).
7. Baker (2011).
8. "... scientists already talk of the dawning of a new geological age, the Anthropocene, named because humans, or rather, the industrial civilization they have created, have become the main factor driving the evolution of Earth." In: 'Stopping a scorcher,' *The Economist*, November 23, 2013, p81.
9. Fleming and Jones refer to CSR as the "opium of the people" for the intoxicating, but in their eyes misleading, prospect this idea holds for meaningful change within the current economic system. See: Peter Fleming & Marc T. Jones, *The End of Corporate Social Responsibility: Crisis & Critique*, Sage Publications, Inc., 2013, p. 67.

10. See: David Chandler & William B. Werther, (3rd edition), *Strategic Corporate Social Responsibility: Stakeholders, Globalization, and Sustainable Value Creation*, Sage Publications, Inc., 2014.

11. Devinney (2009).

12. In December 2013, the American Customer Satisfaction Index released data correlating firms' customer service scores with their subsequent stock market performance, "suggesting that the most-hated companies perform better than their beloved peers. … there's no statistical relationship between customer-service scores and stock-market returns. … If anything, it might hurt company profits to spend money making customers happy." Quoted in: Eric Chemi, 'Proof that it pays to be America's Most-hated Companies,' *Bloomberg Businessweek*, December 17, 2013, http://www.businessweek.com/articles/2013-12-17/proof-that-it-pays-to-be-americas-most-hated-companies

13. For details on studies analyzing the relationship between CSR and firm performance, see: Joshua D. Margolis & James P. Walsh, 'Misery Loves Companies: Rethinking Social Initiatives by Business,' *Administrative Science Quarterly*, Vol. 48, Issue 2, 2003, pp. 268-305; Marc Orlitzky, Frank L. Schmidt, & Sara L. Rynes, 'Corporate Social and Financial Performance: A Meta-analysis,' *Organization Studies*, Vol. 24, Issue 3, 2003, pp. 403–441; and Herman Aguinis & Ante Glavas, 'What We Know and Don't Know About Corporate Social Responsibility: A Review and Research Agenda,' *Journal of Management*, Vol. 38, Issue 4, 2012, pp. 932–968.

14. McEachran (2013).

15. Baker (2008).

16. The work that Walmart (and other retailers) is doing to create a standardized "sustainability index" that would allow comparisons of the ecological footprint across all its products carries the potential to revolutionize the way that we measure CSR. For more information, see The Sustainability Consortium: http://www.sustainabilityconsortium.org/

17. See: Timothy M. Devinney, 'Is the Socially Responsible Corporation a Myth? The Good, the Bad, and the Ugly of Corporate Social Responsibility,' *Academy of Management Perspectives*, Vol. 23, 2009, pp. 44–56.

18. See: Mallen Baker, 'Should CSR be made compulsory after all?' April 17, 2014, http://www.mallenbaker.net/csr/page.php?Story_ID=2800

19. See: David Grayson & Adrian Hodges, 'Corporate Social Opportunity! Seven Steps to Make Corporate Social Responsibility Work for your Business,' *Greenleaf Publishing*, July, 2004.

20. Johnson (1953).

21. Chaplier (2014).

22. "Subterranean capitalist blues" (2013).

23. Norris (2014).

24. For insight into the futility of misaligned incentives that seek to subvert human nature, see: Steven Kerr, 'On the Folly of Rewarding A, While Hoping for B,' *Academy of Management Journal*, Vol. 18, No. 4, 1975, pp. 769–783.

25. See: David Chandler & William B. Werther, (3rd edition), *Strategic Corporate Social Responsibility: Stakeholders, Globalization, and Sustainable Value Creation*, Sage Publications, Inc., 2014.

26. For example, see: Jean Garner Stead & W. Edward Stead, *Sustainable Strategic Management* (2e), M.E.Sharpe, 2013, & Bryan W. Husted & David Bruce Allen, *Corporate Social Strategy: Stakeholder Engagement and Competitive Advantage*, Cambridge University Press, 2010.

27. Freeman, Harrison, Wicks, Parmar, and de Colle (2010).

28. Bowen (1953).

29. For a discussion on this issue, see: R.H. Coase, 'The Problem of Social Cost,' *Journal of Law and Economics*, Vol. 3, Issue 1, 1960, pp. 1–44.

30. For an understanding of this concept as originally constructed, see: Jean Jacques Rousseau, 'The Social Contract: Or Principles of Political Right,' public domain, 1762 (translated in 1782 by G.D.H. Cole).

31. "Does the Good Outweigh the Bad? Sizing up 'Selective' Corporate Social Responsibility" (2013).

32. McWilliams, Siegel, and Wright (2006).

Principle 1

1. Micklethwait and Wooldridge (2003).

2. Confino (2013).

3. Devinney (2009).

4. Micklethwait and Wooldridge (2003).

5. Polman (2014).

6. Bowen (1953).

7. Blount (2014).

8. This debate is heavily influenced, of course, by the ultimate goal that the minimum wage seeks to achieve. Is its primary purpose to price labor (an economic function) or is it to reduce poverty (a social welfare function)? It is most effective as a measure of economic value. If the underlying goal is to reduce poverty, however, economists agree that policies such as the earned income tax credit (a negative income tax for workers on low pay) is a much more effective means of achieving that. For more information, see: 'Deal or no deal?' *The Economist*, February 1, 2014, p8 and 'Making the Economic Case for More Than the Minimum Wage,' *Bloomberg Businessweek*, February 13, 2014, http://www.businessweek.com/articles/2014-02-13/making-the-economic-case-for-more-than-the-minimum-wage

9. Walmart is often criticized for paying below market wage rates. In reality, however, the firm routinely receives applications that are many multiples the number of job openings available (which indicates above market wages). At the extreme, for example, in 2013, when the firm opened a store in Washington D.C., it received more than 23,000 applications for the 600 positions it was advertising—an acceptance rate of 2.6 percent which, it was noted, is "more difficult than getting into Harvard [which] accepts 6.1 percent of applicants." See: Ashley Lutz, 'Applicants For Jobs At The New DC Walmart Face Worse Odds Than People Trying To Get Into Harvard,' *Business Insider*, November 19, 2013, http://www.businessinsider.com/wal-mart-receives-23000-applications-2013-11

10. Burlingham (1989).

Principle 2

1. It is commonly understood that the original purpose of incorporation (by crown charter) was to accomplish continuity of life (beyond that of the original mix of an organization's investors). Limited liability was achieved over time by a legal sleight of hand, redrafting investor obligations in relation to calls for additional capitals. If a bankrupt company had an enforceable right to call in capital from investors, for example, to shore up the continued viability of an enterprise, creditors could claim that right as an asset of the firm and pursue the call (by right of subrogation). Gradually, lawyers began excluding these obligations, with the result that there was no legal claim for creditors to use, thus, by definition, limiting the investors' liability. Once established and accepted, limited liability gained its own legitimacy as an inducement to investors to support entrepreneurs in the value creation process.

2. Subhabrata Bobby Banerjee, 'Corporate Social Responsibility: The Good, the Bad and the Ugly,' *Critical Sociology*, Vol. 34, Issue 1, 2008, p. 53.

3. For a thorough discussion of the founding of the modern-day corporation and, in particular, the construction of the concept of limited liability, see: John Micklethwait & Adrian Wooldridge, *The Company: A Short History of a Revolutionary Idea*, The Modern Library, 2003.

4. Micklethwait and Wooldridge (2003).

5. It is important to note that this discussion relates primarily to the ownership and purpose of publicly traded corporations in the United States. Although there are similarities, corporate law naturally varies across countries and cultures. And, even in the United States, legal precedent governing firms differs among states and based on whether they are private or closely held. This can be seen in *Revlon Inc. v. MacAndrews & Forbes Holdings, Inc.*, 506 A.2d 173 (Del. 1986), a case of limited application in which the Delaware

Supreme Court announced, "where the company was being 'broken up' and shareholders were being forced to sell their interests in the firm to a private buyer, the board had a duty to maximize shareholder wealth by getting the highest possible price for the shares." See: Lynn A. Stout, 'Why We Should Stop Teaching *Dodge v. Ford*,' *Virginia Law & Business Review*, Vol. 3, No. 1, 2008, p. 172.

6. Lipton and Savitt (2007).

7. Berle and Means (1932).

8. "Rise of the distorporation" (2013).

9. Davidoff (2014).

10. "Fast times" (2014).

11. For a detailed exposition of how high-frequency traders utilize technology to exploit arbitrage opportunities in the market and trade on the intentions of other investors, see: Michael Lewis, *Flash Boys: A Wall Street Revolt*, W. W. Norton & Company, 2014. In essence: "High-frequency trading firms would post the 'best price' for every stock and then when hit with a trade, knowing there was a buyer in the market, take advantage of the fragmentation of exchanges and dark pools and latency (high-frequency traders can get to an exchange faster than you) to buy up shares from other HFTs or from Wall Street dark pools, and then nudge the price up and sell those shares. In other words, front run the customer. … It's sleazy and maybe even illegal, akin to nanosecond-scale insider trading." In: Andy Kessler, 'High-Frequency Trading Needs One Quick Fix,' *The Wall Street Journal*, June 16, 2014, p. A15.

12. "Fast times" (2014).

13. "The monolith and the markets" (2013).

14. "The monolith and the markets" (2013).

15. Keynes (1936).

16. Krugman (2014).

17. Bowen (1953).

18. Oxford English Dictionary (2014), Merriam-Webster (2014).

19. While a number of U.S. state corporate codes contain language that defines *shareholders* as the owners of *shares*, which are "the units into which the proprietary interests in a corporation are divided" (e.g., Colorado Corporation Code, Section 7-101-401, http://tornado.state.co.us/gov_dir/leg_dir/olls/sl1993/sl_191.pdf), Delaware, "the single most important [U.S.] state for corporate law purposes … does not define the term stock or otherwise say what it represents. … The Delaware statute is simply silent on the issue of ownership." Julian Velasco, 'Shareholder Ownership and Primacy,' *University of Illinois Law Review*, Vol. 2010, No. 3, 2010, pp. 929-930. Due to this inconsistency in statutory law, it is fair to conclude that the essence

of *ownership* lies in how corporate law is enforced (in other words, what it means in reality) and, in particular, how it is enforced in Delaware. In other words, how courts interpret the relationship between corporations and shareholders, and apply that interpretation to decide the overall direction of the firm, is the ultimate determinant of who legally *owns* the corporation.

20. Lan and Heracleous (2010).

21. For related work that builds on the argument that the firm has obligations to its stakeholders, broadly defined, see: James E. Post, Lee E. Preston, & Sybille Sachs, *Redefining the Corporation: Stakeholder Management and Organizational Wealth*, Stanford Business Books, 2002 and Sybille Sachs & Edwin Ruhli's book, *Stakeholders Matter: A New Paradigm for Strategy in Society*, Cambridge University Press, 2012.

22. Wolf (2014).

23. Fama (1980).

24. Lan and Heracleous (2010).

25. "And what was particularly grotesque about this was that the 14th amendment was passed to protect newly-freed slaves. So, for instance, between 1890 and 1910, there were 307 cases brought before the Court under the 14th amendment—288 of these brought by corporations; 19 by African–Americans. [As a result of the Civil War] 600,000 people were killed to get rights for people and then, with strokes of the pen over the next 30 years, judges applied those rights to capital and property, while stripping them from people." See: *The Corporation* documentary, 2003, http://www.thecorporation.com/

26. In reality, the detail of which rights and responsibilities should be legally ascribed to corporations and which should be reserved for humans alone is an ongoing constitutional debate. As a result, corporations are neither fully fledged individuals, nor are they artificial entities devoid of rights— legal precedent has determined they fall somewhere in between: "In the past, Supreme Court opinions have recognized the need for differing approaches to the recognition (or not) of constitutional rights of business corporations in various settings. For example, the Court has decided that the constitutional protection against 'double jeopardy' for an alleged crime covers organizational persons (such as a corporation), but the right protecting against forcible 'self-incrimination' does not. Similarly, the Court has recognized a right of political free speech for organizations in *Citizens United*, but not 'rights to privacy' which have been reserved for individual human beings. In other words, the Court finds some constitutional rights make sense to extend to organizational persons, and it leaves others to cover only individual people." Quoted from: Eric W. Orts, 'The 'Hobby Lobby' Case: Religious Freedom, Corporations and Individual Rights,' *Knowledge@*

Wharton, March 31, 2014, https://knowledge.wharton.upenn.edu/article/hobby-lobby-case-religious-freedom-corporations-individual-rights/

27. Jonathan R. Macey, 'A Close Read of an Excellent Commentary on *Dodge v. Ford*,' *Virginia Law & Business Review*, Vol. 3, No. 1, 2008, p. 180.

28. Macey (2008).

29. Lublin and Francis (2014).

30. Lublin and Francis (2014).

31. Lublin and Francis (2014).

32. *HL Bolton (Engineering) v TJ Graham and Sons Ltd.* (1957).

33. *Dodge v. Ford Motor Co.*, (1919).

34. For additional insight on this case and why it has historically been misinterpreted as support for the idea the directors of a firm have a fiduciary responsibility to maximize shareholder value, see: Stout, Lynn A., 'Why We Should Stop Teaching *Dodge v. Ford*,' *UCLA School of Law*, Law-Econ Research Paper No. 07–11, 2008.

35. Moreover, because investors are not one homogenous group with similar goals, investment timeframes, and values (they include pension funds, day-traders, and high-frequency computer algorithms), they cannot approximate the legal or actual influence of a sole proprietor who owns 100 percent of a firm's shares (or even a majority owner).

36. See: The Modern Corporation, "Fundamental rules of corporate law," accessed in April, 2014, http://themoderncorporation.wordpress.com/company-law-memo/

37. For example, see: Jacob M. Rose, 'Corporate Directors and Social Responsibility: Ethics versus Shareholder Value,' *Journal of Business Ethics*, Vol. 73, Issue 3, July 2007, pp. 319–331. This study reports that "directors … sometimes make decisions that emphasize legal defensibility at the expense of personal ethics and social responsibility. Directors recognize the ethical and social implications of their decisions, but they believe that current corporate law requires them to pursue legal courses of action that maximize shareholder value." (p. 319).

38. In the business school, we are largely oblivious to this debate that is occurring in the academic corporate law community. For more information, see: http://themoderncorporation.wordpress.com/company-law-memo/

39. Velasco (2010).

40. The corporate legal scholars who authored the statement, the "Fundamental rules of corporate law" at The Modern Corporation, http://themoderncorporation.wordpress.com/company-law-memo/ (accessed in April, 2014), argue that this absence of a fiduciary responsibility of directors is "applicable in almost all jurisdictions."

41. For a detailed examination of the legal foundation (or lack of) for the idea that the primary fiduciary responsibility of the firm's executives and directors is to serve the interests of the firm's shareholders, see: Stout, Lynn (2012). *The Shareholder Value Myth: How Putting Shareholders First Harms Investors, Corporations, and the Public*. San Francisco, CA: Berrett-Koehler Publishers, Inc.

42. See: The Modern Corporation, "Fundamental rules of corporate law," accessed in April, 2014, http://themoderncorporation.wordpress.com/company-law-memo/

43. Lan and Heracleous (2010).

44. *Dodge v. Ford Motor Company* (1919).

45. Stout (2008).

46. "*Dodge v. Ford* is best viewed as a case that deals not with directors' duties to maximize shareholder wealth, but with controlling shareholders' duties not to oppress minority shareholders. The one Delaware opinion that has cited *Dodge v. Ford* in the last thirty years, *Blackwell v. Nixon*, cites it for just this proposition." In: Lynn A. Stout, 'Why We Should Stop Teaching *Dodge v. Ford*,' *Virginia Law & Business Review*, Vol. 3, No. 1, 2008, p. 168.

47. Stout (2008).

48. Stout (2012).

49. An indirect attempt to rebut Stout's arguments was made by Leo E. Strine, Jr., Chief Justice of the Delaware Supreme Court, in an essay in the *Columbia Law Review* ("Can We Do Better by Ordinary Investors? A Pragmatic Reaction to the Dueling Ideological Mythologists of Corporate Law," Vol. 114, Issue 2, pp. 449–502). The essay is primarily a response to the idea of the firm as a "shareholder-driven direct democracy" (p449), which advocates for wider shareholder powers and more frequent shareholder votes to govern firm policy. In arguing against this model, Strine also addresses the "skeptics [who] go so far as to deny that boards of directors must, within the constraints of the law, make the best interests of stockholders the end goal of the governance of a for-profit corporation" (p452). Unfortunately, however, Strine fails to acknowledge the near impossible task of defining what those "interests" might be (given that the firm's stockholders include high-frequency traders holding positions for microseconds, day-traders, and pension funds). He also bases his case on facts such as "only stockholders get to elect directors" (p453), as if that depicts ownership, without acknowledging that, in reality, shareholders vote on the candidates nominated by management and that additional *legal rights* are constrained because many votes (e.g., shareholder resolutions) are non-binding. Most damagingly, by undermining the idea of the direct democracy model (which would at least be more consistent with the idea of shareholders as owners) by arguing that "the best way to ensure that corporations generate wealth for diversified stockholders

is to give the managers of corporations a strong hand to take risks and implement business strategies without constant disruption by shifting stock market sentiment," Strine essentially reinforces Stout's case that the Courts tend to favor management over stockholders in any dispute.

50. Macey (2008).

51. Norris (2014).

52. Loizos Heracleous & Luh Luh Lan, 'The Myth of Shareholder Capitalism,' *Harvard Business Review*, April, 2010, p24. See also: Luh Luh Lan & Loizos Heracleous, 'Rethinking Agency Theory: The View from Law,' *Academy of Management Review*, Vol. 35, No. 2, 2010, pp. 294–314.

53. Although, most of us are shareholders in that we are invested in pension funds that hold shares; in reality, this relationship is indirect since these assets are managed by others on our behalf. Most people would not describe themselves primarily as a shareholder and, often, have a greater proportion of their total wealth invested in other assets, such as property.

54. It is important to draw a distinction between *rights* and *influence*. If executives believe shareholders own the firm, they will respond to their demands. This is true whether or not shareholders actually own the firm. It is interesting to ask, however, that: If shareholders have no legal power, how is this pressure manifested or felt, especially if the firm is not seeking additional capital? One answer highlights the extent to which executive compensation is increasingly tied to firm performance, which is often measured by share price. While this effect helps align the interests of executives and shareholders, it is not clear that the results benefit the long-term interests of the firm. See: Justin Fox & Jay W. Lorsch, 'What Good Are Shareholders?' *Harvard Business Review*, July-August, 2012, pp. 49–57.

55. Chesebrough and Sullivan (2013).

56. There are two ways that a firm can redistribute profits to its shareholders—share buybacks or dividends. While both methods ultimately raise the firm's share price, buybacks raise it directly (by decreasing the number of shares outstanding), while dividends do it indirectly (by making the shares a more attractive investment). The ratio of share buybacks to dividends among U.S. firms is approximately 1:0.62. This figure is calculated using third quarter figures for 2013, during which "U.S. companies in the S&P 500-stock index bought back $128.2 billion of their own shares. ... Combined, stock buybacks and dividends totaled $207 billion." Steven Russolillo, 'Companies Binge on Share Buybacks,' *The Wall Street Journal*, December 24, 2013, p. C1.

57. "Reform school for bankers" (2013).

58. It is also worth noting that shareholder pressure is not the only reason that firms focus on the short term. Executive compensation packages that rely

disproportionately on share price as an indicator of firm performance also have the same effect. As noted by Robert Pozen of Harvard Business School, "At present, most firms distribute case bonuses and stock grants on the basis of the prior year's results. This approach does encourage top executives to favor short-term results over long-term growth." Robert C. Pozen, 'The Misdirected War on Corporate Short-Termism,' *The Wall Street Journal*, May 19, 2014, http://online.wsj.com/news/articles/SB100014240527023045477045 79564390935661048

59. Millman (2014).

60. Velasco (2010).

61. In game theory, this concept of the likelihood of repeat or future interactions has been termed the "shadow of the future." See: Robert Axelrod, *The Evolution of Cooperation*, Basic Books, 1984.

62. See: Elizabeth Rigby & JennyWiggins, 'Unilever Chief Executive Rules out Return to Issuing Financial Targets,' *Financial Times*, May 7, 2009, http://www.ft.com/cms/s/0/c49d164c-3a9e-11de-8a2d-00144feabdc0.html. As Unilever's CEO stated, "At Unilever, … we have moved away from quarterly profit reporting; since we don't operate on a 90-day cycle for advertising, marketing, or investment, why do so for reporting?" In: Paul Polman, 'The remedies for capitalism,' *McKinsey & Company*,

63. See Unilever's Sustainable Living campaign, http://www.unilever.com/sustainable-living/

64. "How far can Amazon go?" (2014).

65. An important step in the transition from shareholder focus to stakeholder focus is for the firm to prioritize its stakeholders (see Principle 3). In the process, firms should understand that a shareholder perspective and a stakeholder perspective are not alternatives, but are different shades of the same perspective. Although many commentators talk in terms of a choice between independent constructs; in reality, this is a forced dichotomy. Since shareholders are also stakeholders, a shareholder perspective is actually just a stakeholder perspective with a narrow focus on one stakeholder (shareholders) instead of many.

Principle 3

1. Although, in management theory, these ideas are best captured by stakeholder theory; in corporate law and economics, a similar effect is described using the concept of *team production*. Team production theory applies in the case of team production problems, which "are said to arise in situations where a productive activity requires the combined investment and coordinated effort of two or more individuals or groups." Team production theory

is applied to corporations as a result of "the observation—generally accepted even by corporate scholars who adhere to the principal-agent model—that shareholders are not the only group that may provide specialized inputs into corporate production." In: Margaret M. Blair & Lynn A. Stout, 'A Team Production Theory of Corporate Law,' *Virginia Law Review*, Vol. 85, No. 2, March 1999, pp. 249, 250.

2. For a more complete exposition of the ideas contained in this section, see: David Chandler & William B. Werther, (3rd edition), *Strategic Corporate Social Responsibility: Stakeholders, Globalization, and Sustainable Value Creation*, Sage Publications, Inc., Chapter 2, 2014.

3. Freeman (1984).

4. Pierce (1945), quoted in: Bowen (1953).

5. Abrams (1951).

6. Bowen (1953).

7. Rhenman (1964). See also Freeman et al. (2010).

8. Freeman (1984).

9. It is important to note that, while anyone who considers themselves a stakeholder can be thought of as such, the firm also plays an important role in identifying those stakeholders it considers important (as implied by the Freeman definition). In other words, it is conceivable that there are stakeholders who might not consider themselves as such, but the company treats them as a stakeholder as a result of its operations or strategic interests.

10. It is interesting to debate whether the natural environment, as a nonindependent actor, should be included as an identifiable stakeholder of the firm. Many argue that it should and that, in fact, the environment has rights that should be protected by law. Others, however, argue that it should not be included because it is not the environment itself that speaks or feels or acts; rather, it is how the degradation of the environment affects other stakeholder groups (e.g., NGOs or the government) who then advocate on its behalf. One argument for including the environment as one of the firm's societal stakeholders is to reinforce the importance of sustainability within the CSR debate, while recognizing that the environment requires actors to speak and act on its behalf in order to be protected.

11. For a network-based stakeholder perspective, see: James E. Post, Lee E. Preston, & Sybille Sachs, 'Managing the Extended Enterprise: The New Stakeholder View,' *California Management Review*, Vol. 45 Issue 1, 2002, pp. 6–28.

12. Bowen (1953).

13. Mackey (2013).

14. Mackey (2011).

15. Likierman (2006).

16. Smith (2012).

17. An important contribution to this debate was made by Mitchell, Agle, and Wood's framework of "stakeholder salience," which helps greatly in identifying the stakeholders that, potentially, pose a threat to the firm (see: Ronald K. Mitchell, Bradley R. Agle, & Donna J. Wood, 'Toward a Theory of Stakeholder Identification and Salience: Defining the Principle of Who and What Really Counts,' *Academy of Management Review*, Vol. 22, Issue 4, 1997, pp. 853–886). Essentially, this model identifies the characteristics that render a stakeholder more or less salient to managers (power, legitimacy, and urgency). While important, stakeholder characteristics are only one of the factors that determine whether a firm should respond to a claim. Equally important are the characteristics of the firm (i.e., strategic relevance) and the characteristics of the issue (i.e., emerging or institutionalized). Mitchell et al. address these factors somewhat with their dimension of "urgency" (and also their idea of managers as a moderator of salience), but are not very specific about why or when something would be urgent. In reality, it is the intersection of all three factors (issue, stakeholder, and organization) that provides a clearer roadmap for managers as to when the firm should act. More specifically, Mitchell et al. never really talk about prioritizing among competing interests. In other words, their model helps identify which stakeholders are important, but provides no real guidance as to which stakeholder the firm should support when their interests conflict.

18. Zadek (2004).

19. Zadek (2004), p. 127.

20. Zadek (2004).

21. Sachs (2014).

22. For a graphical representation of these ideas, see Chandler and Werther (2014).

Principle 4

1. For an extended discussion of this issue, see: T. M. Devinney, P. Auger, & G. M. Eckhardt, *The Myth of the Ethical Consumer*, Cambridge University Press, 2010.

2. For an example of the dangers associated with being too socially responsible, the story of Malden Mills and its Polartec line of clothing is instructive. See: Rebecca Leung, 'The Mensch of Malden Mills,' *60 Minutes, CBS*, July 6, 2003, http://www.cbsnews.com/news/the-mensch-of-malden-mills/. See also, Gretchen Morgenson, 'GE Capital vs. the Small-Town Folk Hero,' *New York Times*, October 24, 2004, p. BU5.

3. The Merriam Webster dictionary, for example, defines the term *responsibility* as "moral, legal, or mental *accountability*," while the Oxford English Dictionary

defines it as "the state or fact of being *accountable*" (emphasis added, see: http://www.merriam-webster.com/dictionary/ and http://www.oed.com/).

4. For a discussion on the cognitive constraints that limit stakeholders' ability or willingness to hold firms to account, see: Michael L. Barnett, 'Why Stakeholders Ignore Firm Misconduct: A Cognitive View,' *Journal of Management*, Vol. 40, Issue 3, 2014, pp. 676–702.

5. See also: David Chandler, 'Why Aren't We Stressing Stakeholder Responsibility?' *Harvard Business Review Blog*, 2010, http://blogs.hbr.org/2010/04/why-arent-we-stressing-stakeho/ and David Chandler, 'Corporate Stakeholder Responsibility?' *Systems of Exchange* blog, 2013, http://systemsofexchange.org/2013/05/corporate-stakeholder-responsibility/

6. Bader (2014).

7. Matthews (2013).

8. Bowen (1953).

9. Reinhardt et al. (2010).

10. While a reasonable response to this statement is that the relationship between company and consumer is iterative (a sort of chicken and egg argument with an unclear origin); given that firms are less able to predict market trends than they are able to respond to those trends, it seems clear that the preeminent direction of influence is from consumer to company (and not the other way around).

11. Bowen (1953).

Principle 5

1. Korngold (2014).

2. Brooks (2014).

3. For an important historical and anthropological perspective on the role of the market as a medium for economic exchange (as well as possible alternatives), see: Karl Polanyi, *The Great Transformation: The Political and Economic Origins of Our Time*, Beacon Press, 1944.

4. Hayek (1988).

5. Authers (2013).

6. Korngold (2014).

7. Friedman (1979).

8. Stiglitz (2014).

9. Madison (1788).

10. "A recent groundbreaking study found that undetected insider trading occurs in a stunning one-fourth of public-company deals." In: Editorial, 'The Hidden Cost of Trading Stocks,' *The New York Times*, June 23, 2014, p. A18.

11. For two excellent social psychology sources that discuss the bounded rationality of humans and the biases and heuristics that we apply in the absence of *rationality*, see: Herbert A. Simon, *Administrative Behavior: A Study of Decision-Making Processes in Administrative Organization*, The Free Press, 1976 and Daniel Kahneman, *Thinking, Fast and Slow*, Farrar, Straus and Giroux, 2011.

12. Rattner (2013).

13. Rattner (2013).

14. "Valuing the long-beaked echidna" (2014).

15. "Valuing the long-beaked echidna" (2014).

16. "The colour of pollution" (2014).

17. For a detailed consideration of the limits of federal government in the U.S., see: Peter H. Schuck, *Why Government Fails So Often*, Princeton University Press, 2014. For example, Schuck argues that, in order to be successful, "a public policy has to get six things right: incentives, instruments, information, adaptability, credibility and management. The federal government tends to be bad at all of these." And, where government intervention proved most successful, it was because bureaucrats "did not try to manage success so much as establish the circumstances for it." Quoted in: Yuval Levin, 'Open Door Policies,' *The Wall Street Journal*, June 10, 2014, p. A13.

18. Bowen (1953).

19. "The logical floor" (2013).

20. Tierney (2011).

21. Tierney (2011).

22. See: http://strategiccsr-sage.blogspot.com/2012/09/strategic-csr-prius-fallacy.html

23. Tierney (2011).

24. Obloj (2013).

25. "Of bongs and bureaucrats" (2014).

26. "The logical floor" (2013).

27. Sainsbury (2013).

28. Smith (1776).

29. Gopnik (2010).

30. Kahneman (2011).

31. Kahneman (2011).

32. Thaler and Sunstein (2009).

33. "Nudge, nudge, think, think" (2012).

34. "Nudge, nudge, think, think" (2012).

35. Brooks (2011).

36. Wansink, Just and McKendry (2010).

37. Boudreaux (2013).

38. Boudreaux (2013).
39. Boudreaux (2013).
40. Frederick (1960).
41. Mankiw (2014).

Principle 6

1. Bowen (1953).
2. Bowen (1953).
3. Jensen (2002).
4. George (2014).
5. Wyatt (2013).
6. Bowen (1953).
7. Bowen (1953).
8. A control group is a separate group that undergoes the same experiment and is, essentially, exactly the same as the test group, apart from one variable (which is the variable of interest to the researcher—in this case, it would be the policy or practice that the executive believes maximizes performance).
9. Skidelsky (2013).
10. Bowen (1953).
11. Jensen (2002).
12. Jensen (2002).

Principle 7

1. "The gated globe" (2013).
2. "The gated globe" (2013).
3. "Scrap them" (2014).
4. From 2009–2011, for example, the U.S. federal government "issued 106 new regulations each expected to have an economic impact of at least $100m a year." See: 'Schumpeter, 'Not open for business,' *The Economist*, October 12, 2013, p. 78.
5. Ybarra (2012).
6. Adam Smith published *The Wealth of Nations* in 1776, but it is his book, *The Theory of Moral Sentiments* (first published in 1759), that leads many observers to describe Smith as a moral philosopher, rather than an economist. For example, see: James R. Otteson, 'Adam Smith: Moral Philosopher,' The Freeman Ideas on Liberty, Vol. 50, Issue 11, November, 2000, http://www.thefreemanonline.org/features/adam-smith-moral-philosopher/
7. "The Corporate Welfare State" (2011).

8. Krugman (2011).

9. Krugman (2011).

10. Wagner (2011).

11. Keynes (1923).

12. OED website, January 2014, http://www.oed.com/view/Entry/66996?redir ectedFrom=externality#eid.

13. Gore and Blood (2006).

14. Talk (2010).

15. Rich (2013).

16. Eisenstein (2014).

17. For more information on how humans are the only species that creates "toxic waste," see: Paul Hawken, *The Ecology of Commerce: A Declaration of Sustainability*, HarperCollins Publishers, 1993.

18. The advances made by firms such as Interface Carpets demonstrate the efficiencies that are open to firms that understand *waste* as a commodity, rather than a cost. See: http://www.interfaceglobal.com/sustainability/our-progress.aspx

19. Hawken (1993), p. 13.

20. A related concept to lifecycle pricing is the *circular economy*. While lifecycle pricing focuses on ensuring all costs of production and consumption are included in the price charged for a product, the circular economy focuses on eradicating waste by improving the design of products to either be easily repaired, reused, or recycled. For more information, see: http://www.theguardian.com/sustainable-business/circular-economy

21. A Pigovian tax is an instrument designed to remedy a market imperfection by taxing a behavior that generates third-party costs (i.e., an externality) that are otherwise unaccounted for in the market price for the product. A carbon tax is a good example of a Pigovian tax. For more information about Pigovian taxes, see: R.H. Coase, 'The Problem of Social Cost,' *The Journal of Law & Economics*, Vol. III, October 1960, pp. 1–44 & William J. Baumol, 'On Taxation and the Control of Externalities,' *The American Economic Review*, Vol. 62, June 1972, pp. 307–322.

22. For an early discussion of the cost, ethical, interorganizational, and information challenges inherent in adopting a lifecycle management program within the firm, see: Mark Sharfman, Rex T. Ellington, & Mark Meo, 'The Next Step in Becoming 'Green': Life-cycle Oriented Environmental Management,' *Business Horizons*, May-June, 1997, pp. 13–22.

23. For an example, see: Andrew Martin, 'How Green Is My Orange?' *The New York Times*, January 21, 2009, http://www.nytimes.com/2009/01/22/business/22pepsi.html.

24. Hayat (2011).

25. Gunther (2014).

26. Waage (2014).

27. "PUMA Completes First Environmental Profit and Loss Account which values Impacts at €145 million," *PUMA*, November 16, 2011, http://about.puma.com/puma-completes-first-environmental-profit-and-loss-account-which-values-impacts-at-e-145-million/. See also: Richard Anderson, 'Puma first to publish environmental impact,' *BBC News*, May 16, 2011, http://www.bbc.co.uk/news/business-13410397

28. Gunther (2014).

29. See: 'Ray Anderson: Mount Sustainability,' *WatchMojo.com*, October 8, 2009, http://www.youtube.com/watch?v=l_P_V0jk3Ig

30. Anderson (2009).

31. While we have done a better job within the CSR community of holding firms responsible for their supply chain, we seem less willing to apply the same standards to firms further up the distribution chain. Why are extraction firms, for example, not held accountable for subsequent uses of the raw materials they take out of the ground? While there has been some discussion of *conflict diamonds/minerals*, responsibility for the supply chain appears to rest with the firm that sells the finished product, rather than the firm that sold the component parts. This is an issue that has yet to emerge for distributors, but it is not difficult to imagine a day when that happens. If we want to hold GAP, Nike, and Walmart responsible for the actions of other firms far removed from them closer to source, we will one day surely hold extraction firms responsible for the actions of other firms and consumers closer to consumption.

32. For a discussion about the limits of our current economic model based around growth and consumption, see: Tim Jackson, 'New economic model needed not relentless consumer demand,' *Guardian Sustainable Business*, January 18, 2013, http://www.guardian.co.uk/sustainable-business/blog/new-economic-model-not-consumer-demand-capitalism.

33. Flower (2009).

Principle 8

1. For a more detailed discussion of the environmental consequences of an expanding population and a static resource base, see: Garrett Hardin, 'Tragedy of the Commons,' Science, Vol. 162, No. 3859, December 13, 1968, pp. 1243–1248, http://www.sciencemag.org/content/162/3859/1243.full.

2. Pollan (2008).

3. Kessler (2013).

4. Estimate based on total sales from 2007 to 2011 of "more than 466 million CFLs." Source: *2011 Global Sustainability Report: Goals Completed*,

Walmart, accessed January 2014, http://www.walmartstores.com/sites/responsibilityreport/2011/commitments_Goals_Completed.aspx.

5. Hawken (1993).

6. "Our Common Future, Chapter 2: Towards Sustainable Development," *UN Documents*, http://www.un–documents.net/ocf–02.htm

7. In defining the term *sustainability*, I think it is useful to distinguish between the use of *sustainability* as a noun and *sustainable* as an adjective. Although, grammatically, the two words clearly stem from the same core meaning; in practical terms, there is a difference. In most uses of the term sustainability, such as by the media, for example, the intended reference is almost always to the environment. When sustainable is being used to qualify the word *business*, however, (i.e., a sustainable business; a term that can be used interchangeably with *strategic CSR*), the meaning conveyed is closer to the original, broad meaning of a business that will last for a long time.

8. In the U.S., for example, when survey respondents were asked what words they most closely associate with *sustainability*, the most common responses were "words such as 'environmentally friendly,' 'natural,' 'organic,' 'green,' 'recycle' and 'renewable.' … Meanwhile, words such as 'ethical,' 'trust,' 'trustworthy,' 'collaboration,' community' and 'transparency' ranked low in their perceived relationship to sustainability." See: 'Open thread: What does 'sustainable' mean to you?' *Guardian Sustainable Business*, February 3, 2014, http://www.theguardian.com/sustainable-business/sustainable-green-meaning-consumer-open-thread.

9. Baue (2007).

10. Gillis (2014).

11. "Global Greenhouse Gas Emissions Data" (2014).

12. Lepore (2011).

13. "Made to break" (2006).

14. "Talking trash" (2012).

15. Grieder (2013).

16. "Fact and Figures on E–Waste and Recycling" (2013).

17. Scott (2005).

18. Scott (2005).

19. Birchall (2008).

20. Chhabara (2009).

21. For more information, see Walmart's webpage on the Sustainability Index, http://corporate.walmart.com/global-responsibility/environment-sustainability/sustainability-index (accessed January, 2014).

22. Ward (2013).

23. Cardella (2013).

24. Cardella (2013).

25. Cardella (2013).
26. See: T.M. Devinney, P. Auger, & G.M. Eckhardt, *The Myth of the Ethical Consumer*, Cambridge University Press, 2010. Also, this effect is enhanced when action involves "change" because humans instinctively value the status quo and fear the unknown: "According to a study of referendums world-wide, voters almost always reject change: if the campaign starts with opinion evenly balanced, the status quo wins in 80 per cent of cases." Rachel Sylvester, 'Voters always know best, that's why it pays not to ask them,' *The Times* in *The Daily Yomiuri*, October 21, 2012, p. 8.
27. Walker (2008).
28. Clifford and Martin (2011).
29. Crain (2010).
30. For example: "Pound for pound, making a Prius contributes more carbon to the atmosphere than making a Hummer, largely due to the environmental cost of the 30 pounds of nickel in the hybrid's battery. ... If a new Prius were placed head-to-head with a used car, would the Prius win? Don't bet on it. Making a Prius consumes 113 million BTUs. ... A single gallon of gas contains about 113,000 Btus, so Toyota's green wonder guzzles the equivalent of 1,000 gallons before it clocks its first mile. A used car, on the other hand, starts with a significant advantage: The first owner has already paid off its carbon debt. Buy a decade-old Toyota Tercel, which gets a respectable 35 mpg, and the Prius will have to drive 100,000 miles to catch up." In: 'Inconvenient Truths: Get Ready to Rethink What It Means to Be Green,' *Wired Magazine*, May 19, 2008, http://www.wired.com/science/planetearth/magazine/16-06/ff_heresies_intro.
31. Rago (2007).
32. Rago (2007).
33. Livestrong (.n.d.).
34. Rago (2007).
35. In April 2010, an oil well that was owned by BP and operated by Transocean (with support from Halliburton) exploded in the Gulf of Mexico. The explosion killed 11 men and resulted in the largest environmental disaster to have occurred in the U.S.
36. "Gulf of Mexico 'dead zone' predictions feature uncertainty" (2012).
37. The Cuyahoga River in Ohio is famous for catching fire numerous times in the 1950s and 1960s. The river was the focus of a 1969 *Time Magazine* report about the levels of pollution in many U.S. rivers, being described as a river that "oozes, rather than flows." The report prompted public outrage and helped build support for the nascent environmental movement. One outcome was the establishment of the Environmental Protection Agency (a U.S. federal government agency) by President Richard Nixon in 1970. See 'America's

Sewage System and the Price of Optimism,' *Time Magazine*, August 1, 1969, http://content.time.com/time/magazine/article/0,9171,901182,00.html.

38. "Stopping a scorcher" (2013).

39. Corner (2013).

40. Corner (2013).

41. Bowen (1953).

42. For background information about this report, see *Stern Review on the Economics of Climate Change*, HM Treasury, 2006, http://webarchive.nationalarchives.gov.uk/+/http:/www.hm-treasury.gov.uk/sternreview_index.htm

43. Kay (2007).

44. Kay (2007).

45. For example, "The 'polar vortex' that brought freezing weather to North America [in 2014] chipped roughly $3 billion off American output in a week." See: 'The weather report,' *The Economist*, January 18, 2014, p. 76.

46. Davenport (2014).

47. Gunther (2013).

48. Grieder (2013).

49. "Back on top" (2013).

50. http://www.ted.com/talks/jason_clay_how_big_brands_can_save_biodiversity.html

Principle 9

1. Godfrey (2005).

2. McLaughlin (2014).

3. McLaughlin (2014).

4. McLaughlin (2014).

5. Boleat (2014).

6. In this sense, the work of C.K. Prahalad (2004) and Stuart Hart (2005) on delivering goods and services to consumers at the bottom-of-the-pyramid is much closer to the idea of *strategic CSR* because the conceptualization of the developing world as an under-served market (rather than a charitable cause) speaks to the power of business to deliver market-based solutions that address some of society's most intractable problems.

7. A transcript of Gates' remarks, together with a link to a video of his January 24, 2008 speech, can be found at: http://www.gatesfoundation.org/media-center/speeches/2008/01/bill-gates-2008-world-economic-forum

8. See: http://www.gatesfoundation.org/media-center/speeches/2008/01/bill-gates-2008-world-economic-forum

9. Kanellos (2008).

10. McCullagh (2008).

11. Easterly (2008).
12. Yunus (2008).
13. Beattie (2008).
14. Beattie (2008).
15. Porter and Kramer(2011).
16. For additional commentary on Porter and Kramer's ideas, see Webb (2011).
17. Hill (2011).
18. Werther and Chandler (2005).

Principle 10

1. Friedman (1970).
2. Confino (2013).
3. Friedman (1970).
4. Friedman (1970).
5. Handy (2002).
6. Handy (2002).
7. Friedman (1970).
8. Friedman (1970).
9. Carroll (1991).

Conclusion

1. See also: David Chandler & William B. Werther, (3rd edition), *Strategic Corporate Social Responsibility: Stakeholders, Globalization, and Sustainable Value Creation*, Sage Publications, Inc., 2014, Chapter 2, p. 65.
2. For more detail, see: David Chandler & William B. Werther, (3rd edition), *Strategic Corporate Social Responsibility: Stakeholders, Globalization, and Sustainable Value Creation*, Sage Publications, Inc., 2014, Chapter 4, p. 141 & Chapter 5, p. 220.
3. The work of John Mackey (Whole Foods Market) on conscious capitalism (http://consciouscapitalism.org/) is, in many ways, complementary to the argument underlying *strategic CSR*.
4. For additional discussion around the idea that *strategic CSR* represents progressive management, see: Thomas E. Graedel & Braden R. Allenby, *Industrial Ecology and Sustainable Engineering*, Prentice Hall, 2009. The authors are industrial ecologists who argue that there is no such thing as *green management* only *good management*.
5. Firms that understand the powerful motivating force of a values-based business include Zappos, Nike, Whole Foods, and Patagonia. Inspiring people,

however, is difficult and expensive. As such, it appears that most firms employ a thin veil of values to bolster their compliance and avoid alienating anyone (a neutral approach), rather than building their firms around values that inspire their stakeholders (a positive approach). The result demonstrates the difference between those firms that understand the powerful and radical consequences of implementing *strategic CSR* and those that do not.

6. Innovation & Design (2008).
7. Zachary and Yamada (1993).
8. Bowen (1953).
9. Bowen (1953).

References

Abrams, F.W. 1951. "Management's Responsibilities in a Complex World." *Harvard Business Review* 29, no. 3, pp. 29–30.

Aguinis, H., and G. Ante. 2012. "What We Know and Don't Know about Corporate Social Responsibility: A Review and Research Agenda." *Journal of Management* 38, no. 4, p. 933.

Al Gore and D. Blood. March 28, 2006. "For People and Planet." *The Wall Street Journal*, p. A20.

Anderson, R. February, 2009. "The Business Logic of Sustainability." *TED2009*, http://www.ted.com/talks/ray_anderson_on_the_business_logic_of_sustainability

Authers, J. December 23, 2013. "Today's Liquid Markets Are Open to Hayekian Criticism." *Financial Times*, p. 12.

Back on Top. September 21, 2013. *The Economist*, p. 24–25.

Bader, C. April 21, 2014. "Why Corporations Fail to Do the Right Thing." *The Atlantic*. http://www.theatlantic.com/business/archive/2014/04/whymaking-corporations-socially-responsible-is-so-darn-hard/360984/

Baker, M. May 2, 2008. "Ethics and financial performance: The big question—Is there really a business case?" *Ethical Corporation Magazine*, http://www.ethicalcorp.com/content.asp?ContentID=5876

Baker, M. May 17, 2011. *PUMA plucks numbers out of the CO2.* http://www.mallenbaker.net/csr/post.php?id=394

Baker, M. April 17, 2014. "Should CSR Be Made Compulsory after All?" http://www.mallenbaker.net/csr/page.php?Story_ID=2800

Baue, B. June 11, 2007. "Brundtland Report Celebrates 20th Anniversary Since Coining Sustainable Development." *Social Funds*. http://www.socialfunds.com/ news/article.cgi/article2308.html

Beattie, A., February 2, 2008. "Poor Returns." Financial Times, p. 33.

Berle, A.A. and G.C. Means. 1932. *The Modern Corporation and Private Property*, New York, NY: Macmillan Publishers Ltd.

Birchall, J. November 4, 2008. "Big Box looks to Small Packages." *Financial Times*, p. 16.

Blount, S. May 13, 2014. "Yes, the World Needs More MBAs. Here's Why." *Bloomberg Businessweek*, http://www.businessweek.com/articles/2014-05-13/yes-the-world-needs-more-mbas-dot-heres-why

Boleat, M. May 27, 2014. "Inclusive Capitalism: Searching for a Purpose Beyond Profit." *Guardian Sustainable Business*, http://www.theguardian.com/sustainable-business/inclusive-capitalism-purpose-beyond-profit

Boudreaux, D.J. April 24, 2013. "Thank You For Smoking." *The Wall Street Journal*, p. A13.

Bowen, H.R. 1953. *Social Responsibilities of the Businessman*, New York, NY: Harper & Brothers, pp. 4, 26, 34, 41–42, 48, 52, 89–90, 102, 111, 114, 139–140, 146, 227.

Brandeis, L.D. November 23, 1912. "Business—The New Profession." *La Follette's Weekly Magazine* 4, no. 47, p. 7.

Brooks, D. May 20, 2014. "The Big Debate." *The New York Times*. p. A19.

Brooks, D. July 8, 2011. "The Unexamined Society." *The New York Times*, p. A21.

Burlingham, B. April 1, 1989. "The Entrepreneur of the Decade." *Inc. Magazine*, http://www.inc.com/magazine/19890401/5602.html

Cardella, A. February 10, 2013. "Attention, Shoppers." *The New York Times Book Review*, p. 21.

Carroll, A.B. July–August, 1991. "The Pyramid of Corporate Social Responsibility: Toward the Moral Management of Organizational Stakeholders." *Business Horizons*, p. 43.

Chandler, D. and W.B. Werther. 2014. *Strategic Corporate Social Responsibility: Stakeholders, Globalization, and Sustainable Value Creation*. 3rd edition. Thousand Oaks, CA: Sage Publications.

Chaplier, J. February, 2014. "EU to force large companies to report on environmental and social impacts," *Guardian Sustainable Business*, http://www.theguardian.com/sustainable-business/eu-reform-listed-companies-report-environmental-social-impact

Chemi, E. 2013. "Proof That It Pays to Be America's Most-Hated Companies," *Bloomberg Businessweek*. http://www.businessweek.com/articles/ 2013-12-17/proof-that-it-pays-to-be-americas-most-hated-companies.

Chesebrough, D. and R. Sullivan. November 26, 2013. "What can companies do about investor short-termism?" *Ethical Corporation Magazine*. http://www.ethicalcorp.com/stakeholder-engagement/what-can-companies-do-about-investor-short-termism

Chhabara, R. Setpember 7, 2009. "Wal-Mart–Thinking outside the big box." *Ethical Corporation*, http://www.ethicalcorp.com/content.asp?ContentID=6583

Clifford, S., and A. Martin. April 22, 2011. "As Consumers Cut Spending, 'Green' Products Lose Allure." *The New York Times Magazine*, p. B4.

Coase, R.H. 1960. "The Problem of Social Cost." *Journal of Law and Economics* 3, Issue 1, pp. 1–44.

Confino, J. October 2, 2013. "Interview: Unilever's Paul Polman on Diversity,

Purpose and Profits," *Guardian Sustainable Business*. http://www.theguardian. com/sustainable-business/unilver-ceo-paul-polman-purpose-profits

Confino, J. 2013. "Interview: Unilever's Paul Polman on diversity, purpose and profits." *Guardian Sustainable Business*, http://www.theguardian.com/ sustainable-business/unilver-ceo-paul-polman-purpose-profits, (accessed on October 2, 2013).

Corner, A. 2013. "'Every Little Helps' is a Dangerous Mantra for Climate Change." *Guardian Sustainable Business*, http://www.theguardian.com/ sustainable-business/plastic-bags-climate-change-every-little-helps, (accessed on December 13, 2013).

Crain, E. Spring/Summer 2010. "Do Consumers Levy a 'Sustainability Penalty' on Certain Goods?" *McCombs Today*, p. 5.

Dahlsrud, A. 2008. "How Corporate Social Responsibility is Defined: An Analysis of 37 Definitions." *Corporate Social Responsibility and Environmental Management* 15, no. 1, p. 1.

Davenport, C. January 24, 2014. "Threat to Bottom Line Spurs Action on Climate." *The New York Times*, p. A1.

Davidoff, S.M. February 14, 2014. "'S.E.C.'s Review of Trading Will See Some of its Own Work." *The New York Times*, p. B5.

"Deal or No deal?" February 1, 2014. *The Economist*, p. 8

Devinney, T.M. 2009 "Is the Socially Responsible Corporation a Myth? The Good, the Bad, and the Ugly of Corporate Social Responsibility." *Academy of Management Perspectives* 23, no. 2, p. 44, 51, 52.

Dodge v. Ford Motor Co., 1919. 204 Mich. 459, 170 N.W. 668.

"Does the Good Outweigh the Bad? Sizing up 'Selective' Corporate Social Responsibility," *Knowledge@Wharton* http://knowledge.wharton.upenn.edu/ article/does-the-good-outweigh-the-bad-sizing-up-selective-corporate-social-responsibility/ (accessed on June 5, 2013).

Easterly, W.R. February 7, 2008. "Why Bill Gates Hates My Book." *The Wall Street Journal*, p. A18.

Eisenstein, C. "Concern about Overpopulation Is a Red Herring; Consumption's the Problem." *Guardian Sustainable Business*, http://www.theguardian. com/sustainable-business/blog/concern-overpopulation-red-herring-consumption-problem-sustainability, (accessed on March 28, 2014).

EPA data. September 25, 2013. "Fact and Figures on E-Waste and Recycling." *Electronics TakeBack Coalition*, p. 3.

Fama, E.F. 1980. "Agency Problems and the Theory of the Firm." *Journal of Political Economy* 88, no. 2, p. 290.

Fast times. April 5, 2014. *The Economist*, p. 73.

Flower, J. 2009. "Sustainable Goes Strategic." *strategy+business*, no. 54, pp. 7–8.

Frederick, W.C. 1960. "The Growing Concern Over Business Responsibility."

California Management Review 2, no. 4, p. 60.

Freeman, R.E. 1984. *Strategic Management: A Stakeholder Approach.* UK: Cambridge University Press, Pitman, pp. 31–51.

Freeman, R.E., J.S. Harrison, C.A. Wicks, B.L. Parmar, and S. de Colle. 2010. *Stakeholder Theory: The State of the Art*, Cambridge University Press, p. 235.

Friedman, M. 1962. *Capitalism and Freedom*. Chicago, IL: University of Chicago Press, Chapter VIII, p. 133.

Friedman, M. "The Social Responsibility of Business is to Increase its Profits," *The New York Times Magazine*, http://www.colorado.edu/studentgroups/libertarians/issues/friedman-soc-resp-business.html, (accessed on September 13, 1970).

Friedman, M. 1979. *The Donahue Show*, http://www.youtube.com/watch?v=Gap XLpLoZBs

George, J.M. 2004. "Compassion and Capitalism: Implications for Organizational Studies." *Journal of Management* 40, no. 1, p. 5.

Gillis, J. April 14, 2014. "Climate Efforts Falling Short, U.N. Panel Says," *The New York Times*, p. A1.

"Global Greenhouse Gas Emissions Data" January, 2014. *United States Environmental Protection Agency*, http://www.epa.gov/climatechange/ghgemissions/global.html, (accessed on January, 2014).

Godfrey, P.C. 2005. "The Relationship between Corporate Philanthropy and Shareholder Wealth: A Risk Management Perspective." *Academy of Management Review* 30, no. 4, pp. 777–98.

Gopnik, A. 2010. "Market Man." *The New Yorker* 86, no. 32, p. 82.

Grayson, D. and A. Hodges. July, 2004. "Corporate Social Opportunity! Seven Steps to Make Corporate Social Responsibility Work for your Business." *Greenleaf Publishing*.

Grieder, E. December 21–22, 2013. "One Man's Trash Is Another's Trade." *The Wall Street Journal*, p. C9.

"Gulf of Mexico 'dead zone' predictions feature uncertainty." *National Oceanic and Atmospheric Administration* (NOAA), http://www.noaanews.noaa.gov/stories2012/20120621_deadzone.html, (accessed on June 20, 2012).

Gunther, M. "Natural Capital: Breakthrough or Buzzword?" *Guardian Sustainable Business*, http://www.theguardian.com/sustainable-business/natural-capital-nature-conservancy-trucost-dow, (accessed on March 6, 2014).

Gunther, M. September 24, 2013. "Sustainability at McDonald's. Really." http://www.marcgunther.com/sustainability-at-mcdonalds-really/

Handy, C. December, 2002. "What's a Business For?" *Harvard Business Review*, pp. 49–55.

Hawken, P. 1993. *The Ecology of Commerce: A Declaration of Sustainability*. HarperCollins Publishers, p. 4, 5, 13.

Hayat, U. February 7, 2011. "Future Challenges for Sustainable Investing."

Financial Times (FTfm), p. 12.

Hayek, F.A. 1988. The Fatal Conceit: The Errors of Socialism, In *The Collected Works of Friedrich August Hayek*, eds. W. W. Bartley III, Routledge, London, UK, Vol. I, p. 14.

Hill, A. February 22, 2011. "Society and the Right Kind of Capitalism," *Financial Times*, p. 14.

HL Bolton (Engineering) v TJ Graham and Sons Ltd. 1957. 1 QB 159 (Court of Appeal), Denning LJ, p. 172.

How far can Amazon go?. June 21, 2014. *The Economist*, p. 11.

http://www.businessweek.com/stories/2008-06-11/peter-senges-necessary-revolutionbusinessweek-business-news-stock-market-and-financial-advice

http://www.merriam-webster.com/ and http://www.oed.com/

http://www.ted.com/talks/jason_clay_how_big_brands_can_save_biodiversity.html

Husted, B.W. and D.B. Allen. 2010. *Corporate Social Strategy: Stakeholder Engagement and Competitive Advantage.* Cambridge, UK: Cambridge University Press.

Innovation & Design, "Peter Senge's Necessary Revolution," June 11, *Bloomberg Businesseeek*, 2008, Jason Clay TED Talk, July, 2010. http://www.ted.com/talks/jason_clay_how_big_brands_can_save_biodiversity.html

Jensen, M.C. 2002. "Value Maximization, Stakeholder Theory, and the Corporate Objective Function." *Business Ethics Quarterly* 12, no. 2, pp. 239, 245, 253–6.

Johnson, F.E. 1953. "Commentary on the Ethical Implications of the Study," In *Social Responsibilities of the Businessman*, eds. R. Howard and S. Bowen, New York, NY: Harper & Brothers, p. 256.

Kahneman, D. 2011. *Thinking, Fast and Slow.* Farrar, Straus and Giroux: New York, pp. 411–2.

Kanellos, M. "On 'Creative Capitalism,' Gates Gets it." *CNET News.com*, http://www.news.com/On-creative-capitalism%2C-Gates-gets-it/2010-1014_3-6227712.html, (accessed on January 25, 2008).

Kay, J. November 28, 2007. "Climate Change: The (Groucho) Marxist Approach." *Financial Times*, p. 11.

Kessler, A. "Living the California Nanny-State Life." December 28–29, 2013, *The Wall Street Journal*, p. A13.

Keynes, J.M. 1923. *A Tract on Monetary Reform.* Macmillan Publishers, pp. 79–80.

Keynes, J.M. 1936. *The General Theory of Employment, Interest and Money.* New York, NY: Harcourt Brace and Co., p. 156.

Korngold, A. "Business can Do What Governments Can't: Solve the World's Biggest Problems." *Guardian Sustainable Business*, http://www.theguardian.com/sustainable-business/business-government-world-problems-davos-multinational, (accessed on January 7, 2014).

Krugman, P. November 7, 2011. "Here Comes the Sun." *The New York Times*, p. A21.

Krugman, P. May 9, 2014. "Now That's Rich." *The New York Times*, p. A25.

Lan, L.L. and L. Heracleous. 2010. "Rethinking Agency Theory: The View from Law," *Academy of Management Review* 35, no. 2, pp. 300–1.

Lepore, M. "15 Facts About Starbucks That Will Blow Your Mind." *Business Insider*, http://www.businessinsider.com/15-facts-about-starbucks-that-will-blow-your-mind-2011-3, (accessed on March 25, 2011).

Likierman, A. June 16, 2006. "Stakeholder Dreams and Shareholder Realities." Mastering Financial Management, *Financial Times*, p. 10.

Lipton, M. and W. Savitt. 2007. "The Many Myths of Lucian Bebchuk." *Virginia Law Review* 93, no. 3, p. 754.

Livestrong. *Wristbands*. http://store.livestrong.org/wristbands.html

Lublin, J.S. and T. Francis. 2014. "Where Majority Doesn't Rule." *The Wall Street Journal*, p. B8.

Lutz, A. November, 2013. "Applicants For Jobs At The New DC Walmart Face Worse Odds Than People Trying To Get Into Harvard," *Business Insider*. http://www.businessinsider.com/wal-mart-receives-23000-applications-2013-11

Macey, J.R. 2008. "A Close Read of an Excellent Commentary on *Dodge v. Ford*." *Virginia Law & Business Review* 3, no. 1, p. 180, 190.

Mackey, J. October 28, 2011. "Are Companies Responsible for Creating Jobs?" *The Wall Street Journal*, p. B1.

Mackey, J. 2013. "Whole Foods Founder John Mackey on Fascism and 'Conscious Capitalism.'" *National Public Radio*, http://www.npr.org/blogs/thesalt/2013/01/16/169413848/whole-foods-founder-john-mackey-on-fascism-and-conscious-capitalism, (accessed on January 16, 2013).

"Made to Break: Are we Sinking under the Weight of our Disposable Society?" *Knowledge@Wharton*, http://knowledge.wharton.upenn.edu/article.cfm?article id=1536, (accessed on August 9, 2006).

Madison, J. February 6, 1788. "Federalist No.51: The Structure of the Government Must Furnish the Proper Checks and Balances Between the Different Departments."

"Making the Economic Case for More Than the Minimum Wage." February 13, 2014. *Bloomberg Businessweek*. http://www.businessweek.com/articles/2014-02-13/making-theeconomic-case-for-more-than-the-minimum-wage

Mankiw, N.G. March 23, 2014. "When the Scientist Is Also a Philosopher." *The New York Times*, p. BU4.

Margolis, J.D. and J.P. Walsh. 2003. "Misery Loves Companies: Rethinking Social Initiatives by Business. "*Administrative Science Quarterly* 48, Issue 2, pp. 268–305.

Matthews, C.M. "White Re-Kindles Debate on Corporate Penalties." *The*

Wall Street Journal, http://blogs.wsj.com/riskandcompliance/2013/09/30/
the-morning-risk-report-white-re-kindles-debate-on-corporate-penalties/
(accessed on September 30, 2013).

McCullagh, D. "Gates Misses the Point on 'Creative Capitalism." *CNET News.com,*
http://www.news.com/Gates-misses-the-point-on-creative-capitalism/2010
-1014_3-6227726.html, (accessed on January 25, 2008).

McEachran, R. 2013. "Ethical awards: Green wash or genuinely recognising
sustainability." *Guardian Sustainable Business Blog,* http://www.theguardian.
com/sustainable-business/blog/ethical-awards-green-wash-sustainability
(accessed on September 3, 2013).

McLaughlin, G. "Why Brands Should Focus on Social Change, not Philanthropy."
Guardian Sustainable Business, http://www.theguardian.com/sustainable-business
/responsibility-good-business-long-term, (accessed on January 17, 2014),

McWilliams, A., S.D. Siegel, and M.P. Wright. 2006. "Corporate Social
Responsibility: Strategic Implications," *Journal of Management Studies* 43,
no. 1, pp. 1–18.

Micklethwait, J. and A. Wooldridge. 2003. *The Company: A Short History of a
Revolutionary Idea.* The Modern Library, p. 15, 43, 46.

Millman, G.J. May 22, 2014. "Firms See Value Opportunity in Shareholder Base."
The Wall Street Journal, http://blogs.wsj.com/riskandcompliance/2014/05/22/
the-morning-risk-report-companies-see-value-opportunity-in-shareholder-
base/

Norris, F. June 6, 2014. "The Islands Treasured By Offshore Tax Avoiders."
The New York Times, p. B1.

Norris, F. March 21, 2014. "Companies That Lie Increasingly Win in Court."
The New York Times, p. B1.

Nudge, Nudge, Think, Think. March 24, 2012. *The Economist,* p. 78.

Obloj, T. "Financial incentives and bonus schemes can spell disaster for business."
Guardian Sustainable Business, http://www.theguardian.com/sustainable-
business/financial-incentives-bonus-schemes-lloyds-fine, (accessed on December
11, 2013).

Of Bongs and Bureaucrats. January 11, 2014. *The Economist,* p. 11.

"Open thread: What does 'sustainable' mean to you?" 2014. Guardian Sustainable
Business.   http://www.theguardian.com/sustainable-business/sustainable-
greenmeaning-consumer-open-thread, (accessed on February 3, 2014).

Orlitzky, M., F.L. Schmidt, and S.L. Rynes. 2003. "Corporate Social and
Financial Performance: A Meta-Analysis." *Organization Studies* 24, Issue 3,
pp. 403–441.

"Our Common Future," Chapter 2, In *Towards Sustainable Development. UN
Documents,* http://www.un-documents.net/ocf-02.htm

Oxford English Dictionary. 2014. http://www.oed.com/view/Entry/66996?

redirectedFrom=externality#eid

Pierce, F.W. December 6, 1945. 'Developing Tomorrow's Business Leaders,' an address to the Cincinnati Chapter of the Society for the Advancement of Management, quoted in: Bowen, H.R. *Social Responsibilities of the Businessman*. Harper & Brothers, 1953, p. 51.

Pollan, M. April 20, 2008. "Why Bother?" *The New York Times*, p. 19.

Polman, P. "Business, society, and the future of capitalism," *McKinsey Quarterly*, http://www.mckinsey.com/Insights/Sustainability/Business_society_and_the_future_of_capitalism, (accessed on May 2014).

Porter, M.E. and M.R. Kramer. 2011. "Creating Shared Value," *Harvard Business Review*, Vol. 89, p. 64.

Rago, J. March 23, 2007. "Conspicuous Virtue and the Sustainable Sofa." *The Wall Street Journal*, p. W13.

Rattner, S. November 15, 2013. "Who's Right on the Stock Market?" *The New York Times*, p. A25.

Reform school for bankers. October 5, 2013. *The Economist*, p. 73.

Reinhardt, F., R. Casadesus-Masanell, and H.J. Kim, "Patagonia." October 19, 2010. *Harvard Business School*, [9-711-020], p. 8.

Rhenman, E. *Foeretagsdemokrati och foeretagsorganisation*, S.A.F. Norstedt: Företagsekonomiska Forsknings Institutet, Thule, Stockholm, 1964. See also: Freeman, R. E., J. S. Harrison, A. C. Wicks, B. L. Parmar, & S. de and Colle, *Stakeholder Theory: The State of the Art*, Cambridge University Press, 2010, p. 48.

Rich, N. October 13, 2013. "Earth Control." *The New York Times Book Review*, p. 18.

Rousseau, J.J. 1762. "The Social Contract: Or Principles of Political Right." Public domain, (translated in 1782 by G.D.H. Cole).

Rise of the Distorporation. October 26, 2013. *The Economist*, p. 30.

Sachs, J. "The Ultimate Missed Social-media Opportunity for Brands: Climate Change." *Guardian Sustainable Business*, http://www.theguardian.com/sustainable-business/social-marketing-brands-coke-chevrolet-climate-change-environment, (accessed on March 12, 2014).

Sainsbury, D. 2013. *"Progressive Capitalism: How to Achieve Economic Growth, Liberty and Social Justice,"* Biteback, http://www.thersa.org/fellowship/journal/archive/spring-2013/features/the-enabling-state

Scott, L. "Wal-Mart: Twenty First Century Leadership." http://walmartwatch.com/img/documents/21st_Century_Leadership.pdf, (accessed on October 24, 2005).

Scrap Them. June 14, 2014. *The Economist*, p. 14.

Skidelsky, R. November 25, 2013. "4 Fallacies of Fiscal Austerity Debunked." *The Japan News by The Yomiuri Shimbun*, p. 9.

Smith, A. 1776. *The Wealth of Nations*, pp. 11–12.

Smith, H. "When Capitalists Cared." *The New York Times.* http://www.nytimes.com/2012/09/03/opinion/henry-ford-when-capitalists-cared.html, (accessed on September 2, 2012).

Stead, J.G. and W.E. Stead. 2013. *Sustainable Strategic Management.* 2nd ed. Armonk, New York, NY: M.E. Sharpe.

Stiglitz, J.E. June 29, 2014. "Inequality Is Not Inevitable." *The New York Times,* p. SR7.

Stopping a scorcher. November 23, 2013, *The Economist,* p. 80.

Stout, L. 2012. *The Shareholder Value Myth: How Putting Shareholders First Harms Investors, Corporations, and the Public.* Berrett-Koehler Publishers, Inc., San Francisco, CA, pp. 3–4.

Stout, L.A. 2008. "Why We Should Stop Teaching *Dodge v. Ford*," *Virginia Law & Business Review* 3, no. 1, p. 166.

"Subterranean capitalist blues." October 26, 2013. *The Economist,* p. 13.

"Sustainability Index." January, 2014. *Walmart.* http://corporate.walmart.com/global-responsibility/environment-sustainability/sustainability-index

"Talking Trash." June 2, 2012. *The Economist Technology Quarterly,* p. 12.

Thaler, R.H. and C.R. Sunstein. 2009. *Nudge: Improving Decisions About Health, Wealth, and Happiness.* Penguin Books, 2009.

The Colour of Pollution. May 24, 2014. *The Economist,* p. 29.

The Corporate Welfare State, (Editorial). November 7, 2011. *The Wall Street Journal,* p. A18.

The Gated Globe. October 12, 2013. *The Economist,* p. 13.

The Logical Floor. December 14, 2013. *The Economist,* p. 18.

The monolith and the markets. December 7, 2013. *The Economist,* p. 25, 26.

Arizona State University and University of Arkansas. n.d. *The Sustainability Consortium.* http://www.sustainabilityconsortium.org/

Tierney, J. March 7, 2011. "When Energy Efficiency Sullies the Environment." *The New York Times,* p. D1.

Valuing the Long-Beaked Echidna. February 22, 2014. *The Economist,* p. 66.

Velasco, J. 2010. "Shareholder Ownership and Primacy." *University of Illinois Law Review,* no. 3, pp. 899, 901, 902.

Waage, S. "How can the Value of Nature be Embedded in the World of Business?" *Guardian Sustainable Business,* http://www.theguardian.com/sustainable-business/finance-nature-no-value-natural-capital, (accessed on March 31, 2014).

Wagner, G. September 8, 2011. 'Going Green but Getting Nowhere,' *The New York Times,* p. A25.

Walker, R. 2008. "Sex vs. Ethics." *Fast Company Magazine,* 124, pp. 54–6.

Wansink, B., D.R. Just, and J. McKendry. October 22, 2010. "Lunch Line

Redesign." *The New York Times*, p. 35.

Ward, J.I. "Sprint Wins on e-waste: Why Do AT&T and Verizon Fall Short?" *Guardian Sustainable Business*, http://www.theguardian.com/sustainable-business/sprint-wins-waste-phone-companies, (accessed on November 5, 2013).

Wolf, M. "AstraZeneca is more than investors' call." *Financial Times*, http://www.ft.com/cms/s/0/6fe31054-d691-11e3-b251-00144feabdc0.html, (accessed on May 8, 2014).

Wyatt, E. December 30, 2013. "U.S. Struggles to Keep Pace in Delivering Broadband Service." *The New York Times*, p. B1.

Ybarra, M.J. June 11, 2012. "Free to Choose, and Conserve." *The Wall Street Journal*, p. A11.

Zachary, G.P. and K. Yamada, "From 1993: What's Next? Steve Job's Vision, So on Target at Apple, Now Is Falling Short," *The Wall Street Journal*, http://online.wsj.com/news/articles/SB10001424052970203476804576614371332161748, (accessed on May 25, 1993).

Zadek, S. 2004. "The Path to Corporate Responsibility." *Harvard Business Review*, pp. 125–32.

Index

This book is a publication in support of the United Nations Principles for Responsible Management Education (PRME), housed in the UN Global Compact Office. The mission of the PRME initiative is to inspire and champion responsible management education, research and thought leadership globally. Please visit www.unprme.org for more information.

The Principles for Responsible Management Education Book Collection is edited through the Center for Responsible Management Education (CRME), a global facilitator for responsible management education and for the individuals and organizations educating responsible managers. Please visit www.responsiblemanagement.net for more information.

—Oliver Laasch, University of Manchester, Collection Editor

- *Business Integrity in Practice: Insights from International Case Studies* by Agata Stachowicz-Stanusch and Wolfgang Amann
- *Academic Ethos Management: Building the Foundation for Integrity in Management Education* by Agata Stachowicz-Stanusch
- *Responsible Management: Understanding Human Nature, Ethics, and Sustainability* by Kemi Ogunyemi
- *Fostering Spirituality in the Workplace: A Leader's Guide to Sustainability* by Priscilla Berry
- *A Practical Guide to Educating for Responsibility in Management and Business* by Ross McDonald
- *Educating for Values-Driven Leadership: Giving Voice to Values Across the Curriculum* by Mary Gentile, Editor (with 14 contributing authors)
- *Teaching Anticorruption: Developing a Foundation for Business Integrity* by Agata Stachowicz-Stanusch and Hans Krause Hansen
- *Responsible Management Accounting and Controlling: A Practical Handbook for Sustainability, Responsibility and Ethics* by Daniel A. Ette
- *Teaching Ethics Across the Management Curriculum: A Handbook for International Faculty* by Kemi Ogunyemi

Announcing the Business Expert Press Digital Library

*Concise E-books Business Students Need
for Classroom and Research*

This book can also be purchased in an e-book collection by your library as
- a one-time purchase,
- that is owned forever,
- allows for simultaneous readers,
- has no restrictions on printing, and
- can be downloaded as PDFs from within the library community.

Our digital library collections are a great solution to beat the rising cost of textbooks. E-books can be loaded into their course management systems or onto students' e-book readers.

The **Business Expert Press** digital libraries are very affordable, with no obligation to buy in future years. For more information, please visit **www.businessexpertpress.com/librarians**. To set up a trial in the United States, please email **sales@businessexpertpress.com**.